PARENTING TEEN GIRLS

PARENTING TEEN GIRLS

A POSITIVE PARENTING APPROACH TO RAISING HEALTHY, INDEPENDENT DAUGHTERS

CHRISTINA TRUJILLO SIEREN, LCSW

ROCKRIDGE
PRESS

Interior and Cover Designer: Angela Navarra
Art Producer: Meg Baggott
Editor: Barbara J. Isenberg
Production Editor: Ruth Sakata Corley
Production Manager: Martin Worthington

Author photo courtesy of Paige Heuer

Paperback ISBN: 978-1-63807-991-0
eBook ISBN: 978-1-63878-512-5
R0

For Carter Royce and Violet Kennedy. Being your mom has been the most incredible journey. I love you both to the moon and back, to infinity and beyond, and over the rainbow where the unicorns live!

CONTENTS

INTRODUCTION

I'm so excited to be here with you to talk about parenting and some of the ins and outs of adolescent development. While I have expertise within the parenting arena, I also value your role as the parent, caregiver, guardian, and loved one to your teen, and see this book as an opportunity to collaborate with you.

In 2006, as I started my third summer working in a therapeutic program for high-risk children, I was asked to supervise a female adolescent group. I remember being scared, as I'd never worked with adolescents before, and literally everything I'd heard about working with adolescent girls had been unfavorable. Surprisingly, it was one of my most rewarding summers, so much so that from that point forward, I dedicated my career to working with adolescents, including teens who identify as females.

In 2007, I was awarded my master's in social work from the University of Southern California and in 2010 became a licensed clinical social worker in the state of California. Since then, I have worked in community mental health, specialized foster care, academic settings, and currently, a private practice in Santa Clarita, California, where I specialize in working with high-risk adolescents and their families, as well as high-conflict families. Additionally, I'm the lead parenting coach with Unapparent Parenting, Inc., where I coach parents of teens to question parenting myths and reposition themselves with an authentic parenting blueprint that aligns them with their core values and highest priorities, while fueling connection with their teen.

Over the years, I've heard countless stories from both parents and teens regarding the challenges that embody adolescence. Caregivers make every effort to wrap their heads around a developmental period that keeps them on their toes, and teens try to make sense of their growing independence that sometimes feels chaotic and messy. As parents witness the ebb and flow of their teen's growing autonomy, it can be difficult to take a step back and allow the many layers of adolescence to unfold naturally. Even in the best cases, it can be a very challenging time for both parents and teens.

No one prepares us for parenthood, but my hope is that this book will provide you with tips, tools, knowledge, and guidance that support you in more confidently and effectively engaging with your teen. As parents, we don't always get it right, but I believe that some of the most beautiful parenting moments come when we're entering unknown territory and are unsure of what lies ahead. Parenting truly affords countless opportunities to connect and re-connect with your teen.

My goal is to provide you with information that is grounded in research, prioritizes safety, and nourishes the relationship between you and your child. The parenting approaches and tools highlighted throughout this book are based on positive parenting principles, which align with the belief that children are born with good intentions. These principles focus on positive discipline, as opposed to punishment models that are rooted in controlling outcomes and using fear to regulate behaviors. Positive parenting is a method that provides for mutual respect and understanding between parent and child, moving away from parenting tools that cast judgment on choices made by teens and use manipulation and dishonesty.

Just as no two teens are alike, no two parents are the same, which undoubtedly means no two families are alike, either. I invite you to integrate the following chapters in ways that make the most sense for you, your teen, and your family. In doing so, I hope you'll get immense value out of this book.

WHAT IS POSITIVE PARENTING?

Like this book, positive parenting acknowledges "parent" as an inclusive term and honors those individuals who play a caretaking role in the well-being of a child, extending to adoptive and foster parents, grandparents, family members, and any other individual who plays a nurturing and supportive role.

Positive parenting understands that challenges are normal and takes a proactive approach to parenting. In doing so, positive parenting separates itself from a deficit-based model, which focuses on problems and what's lacking. Positive parenting concentrates on protective factors, which we'll discuss, and what's already working within the child and the child-parent dynamic.

Positive parenting believes that all children are born good and want to engage in positive behaviors. It solidifies attachment, empathy, positive discipline, and respect as its foundations. The relationship between the teen and caregiver is at the forefront of this model, and the focus is the best interest of the child. Parenting is provided in a consistent and unconditional manner, respecting the stage of a child's development. Open communication, emotional support, and non-violence are additional values inherent to this approach.

In practice, positive parenting models for teens what we want them to practice in their daily experiences, which naturally asks that loved ones take an active role in parenting. Parents become leaders, teachers, and coaches, modeling effective communication and behaviors; teens become a collaborative partner in their growth, both by taking an active role in navigating their choices and by organically witnessing behaviors and learning approaches they can then emulate. Under this model, parents leave a controlling parenting perspective behind, and learn how to reframe parenting challenges into opportunities for growth, acceptance, and connection. Parenting is constantly evolving, and teens are consistently changing as well—positive parenting understands this. Positive parenting has the capacity to grow with the developing needs of each teen and the individual caregiver, and flows with the unique teen-parent dynamic, empowering both.

5-STEP "EMOTION COACHING"

Endless parenting books and resources exist, yet caregivers are often plagued by indecision over which resource to turn to. Many parenting ideas contradict one another, and recommended approaches don't always adapt to real-life situations. Different factors impact these gaps, and John Gottman, one of the co-founders of the Gottman Institute, observed the need for more research to understand what makes a "good" parent. Turning his focus away from parenting misconceptions, he developed "The Emotion Coach," one of four parenting types that's rooted in an emotional approach to addressing concerning behaviors. Emotion coaching moves away from a "let's fix the behavior" mindset into a "what's the underlying cause for this behavior" mindset.

Here's how it works:

STEP 1 asks that parents pay attention to their own emotions, while also attuning to the emotions of their teen.

STEP 2 is to connect with the teen and recognize that their emotional experiences are all opportunities for learning, and to teach them to talk about their feelings.

STEP 3 includes listening to your teen and respecting what they have to say. This is an opportunity to understand your teen without judgment.

STEP 4 is to name the feelings your teen is feeling and help provide them with an emotional vocabulary by modeling your own emotions. Talking about your own feelings is one way to model.

STEP 5 focuses on collaborative problem-solving, which includes thinking about possible solutions to a given concern.

Emotional coaching takes practice, yet when parents take time to master these steps, both parents and teens have more opportunities to connect by creating an emotional foundation of understanding. Solidifying these steps will allow teens to formulate skills in emotional regulation, which can minimize escalation into bigger behaviors; teens will also come to see that there's a mutual respect with their parental figure.

HOW TO USE THIS BOOK

Before we dive in, I'd like to talk about how this book is organized and what you can expect moving forward, including how and when specific topics will be covered. Each of the eight chapters starts with an overview of what to expect followed by four content sections, and ends with parenting strategies and key takeaways.

Parenting strategies can be found under the heading "Study Prep: Your Positive Parenting Tips." Each chapter contains five or six of these accessible strategies, which you can try with your teen. What's great is that these strategies directly relate back to the chapter's content, so you'll have concrete "how-to" approaches to address the larger topics within each chapter.

Also unique to each chapter are recurring "Taking a Deeper Look" sections. These resemble a question and response format, and each chapter has two questions written from a parent's perspective. The answers provided take an educational approach and include research findings. The goal of these sections is to address challenges that both teens and parents may experience, giving additional insight into how to best support your teen.

This book explores many topics, starting with chapter 1, which covers the larger culture that acts as a backdrop for teens, the pressure teens face trying to fit in, common parenting myths, and the importance of raising empowered females.

Chapter 2 focuses on different biological developments including physical, cognitive, and social changes, with additional attention given to puberty and brain development.

Chapter 3 is all about communication, including how girls tend to speak with peers and adults, the importance of sharing feelings as part of a healthy communication practice, and how girls display forms of direct and indirect aggression. Any modern discussion of communication wouldn't be complete without attention to social media and the inherent pressures that come with different platforms.

Chapter 4 covers different relationships, including friendships and romantic relationships, and provides parents with recommendations on what to do if they believe a peer is a bad influence or if they don't like who their teen has chosen to date.

Next, chapter 5 addresses cyberbullying, also known as online bullying, and warning signs to watch out for. It also covers beauty standards, cutting behaviors, and eating disorders. Chapter 6 focuses on sexual health, sexual intercourse, and birth control methods, and shares research on the importance of talking about sex with your teen and how sex ed in the classroom often falls short of providing a well-rounded and inclusive education.

Chapter 7 addresses gender expression, why teens "try on" different looks, and how aesthetics and creativity play roles in challenging the status quo. And finally, chapter 8 covers alcohol, vaping, and substance use, with a focus on how alcohol impacts brain development and why drinking is appealing for teens.

As you begin, please know that there's no right or wrong way to move through these chapters. Some chapters may read more easily than others; some are more technical, and others are heavy due to the nature of the chapter's content. I encourage you to read at your own pace, and I hope that this information provides insights that will help you further connect with your teen.

CHAPTER 1

A BRIEF HISTORY OF THE TEENAGE GIRL

Parents often say, "Things were different when I was growing up." There's this inherent separation between the experience of the parent and that of their teen. The underlying theme that things have evolved so much makes it seem like teens are unrelatable to parents. Often, this gap is perceived to be larger than it really is. Information tends to be an issue here, whether it's not having enough, not having the right kind, not feeling secure in how the information relates to adolescent development, or wondering how to effectively apply what you know. My hope is that the information here will help close this gap.

IN THIS CHAPTER, WE'LL EXPLORE:

- The cultural factors that impact teens as they're growing up, and what makes teens who they are

- The pull that teens experience between wanting to fit in among peers and their desire to stand out and be unique

- Common parenting myths and why it's important to rethink them

- Gender inequality, how gender discrepancies support the importance of girls being empowered, and how to equip girls with the resources to close the gender gap

- Questions and answers regarding issues teens face today

We'll end with positive parenting tips, offering strategies to help you address some of these topics with your teen.

AN ANTHROPOLOGICAL LOOK AT TEEN CULTURE

It's familiar to hear the characteristics that come with being a teen—awkward, challenging, hormonal, and dramatic are just a few. We've become accustomed to labeling this developmental phase as difficult for both parents and teens, which means that often our efforts center on fixing traits and behaviors that are a normal part of adolescence. Yet, there's a bigger question that lies in the background: What role does culture play during the teen years?

Today's teens face unique pressures. COVID-19, which has resulted in lockdowns, restrictions on social gatherings, and ongoing questions about when things will return to "normal," has changed life for everyone.

Then there's social media. Social media is everywhere, allowing teens to create and share information, observe and absorb content, and engage in social networks unlimited by location. At the click of a button, a teen could expand their social circle nationwide, even worldwide if they wanted to. Most of this activity can be done without parental supervision, leaving teens to navigate and attempt to make sense of all the information and misinformation out there, in addition to a world of people with different types of intentions.

Because social media is so accessible, teens can get up-to-the-minute updates on issues happening around the world. Racial injustice, political unrest, and climate change, to name a few, are issues impacting how teens experience the world around them, as well as how they view themselves within this larger landscape.

Just like adults, teens are trying to make sense of these current events. How does a teen navigate the idea that equal justice doesn't exist for all people, and that some of their fellow humans have been denied certain rights based on race? Or that droughts, heat waves, melting ice, and rising sea levels caused by climate change will affect their future? How do they make sense of a political climate that involves anti-government demonstrations, rioting, and protests? These are heavy questions most adults have trouble comprehending.

The confrontation of these topics presents defining moments in which teens can cement their own beliefs—beliefs they will carry with them—on many issues that were not as apparent even a decade ago. For example, escalating concerns about climate change have teens wondering about their own impact on the environment, as well as how they can take a proactive role to slow the effects of damages done and protect our future planet.

Teens are prioritizing advocacy and inclusivity, and engaging in various topics that support diversity. We see this in discussions around sexual orientation, gender identity, social justice, and race. Compared to generations before, teens have the choice to more openly explore and identify in ways that challenge previous concepts of sexuality and gender.

These modern influences are certainly not an exhaustive list and are distinct to each individual teen and community. It's also necessary to consider religious and spiritual influences, family values and traditions, academic settings, medical and sports affiliations, and connections with community organizations.

The takeaway here is that teens are confronted with profound influences that undoubtedly impact their experience of the world, as well as the defining question, "Who am I?" Without recognizing the backdrop of these larger contexts of the contemporary day, we may be attempting to view teen development from a narrow and outdated lens.

THE STRUGGLE TO BELONG IS JUST AS REAL AS THE DESIRE TO BE UNIQUE

To say that the teen years are pivotal would be a huge understatement; yet to only acknowledge this developmental period as a stage of identifying who teens are and where they fit in would be evasive. The overarching theme falls within the question of "Who am I and where do I belong?"; but additional layers set the stage for the ebb and flow that occur between the desire to belong and a craving to be unique.

As teens experience rapid physical changes and ongoing emotional growth, a desire to belong is at the forefront. As humans, we have an innate need to be connected, and teens are fully engaging in this process. Teens want to be accepted by their peers, and they want validation that they're good enough to belong. This need for approval, coupled with the desire to create a strong identity, requires that teens "try on" different social groups, music tastes, clothing styles, etc., while also testing out opinions and moving between different beliefs.

As teens test the waters of who they are, they are also navigating pressures to fit in; the trouble is, these pressures to be or act in certain ways don't always align with a true sense of belonging. To belong is to feel safe within a group, and to feel pressured signals insecurity due to the potential of not being accepted. Yet, it's common for teens to engage in behaviors that clash with their sense of security, as the need to belong is fueled by the belief "If I do this, they will like me." It's also extremely brave for teens to step away from a group that doesn't align with their growing sense of who they are.

Because teens are developing their fit within a larger society, it is common for them to move between the masks they try on and show others, and the person they truly are behind the mask. To be unique also falls under the umbrella of belonging, as teens want to be unconditionally accepted for their individuality, including that which is different, and the oftentimes contradictory ways they are navigating the world. To truly be seen as the individual they are requires that the masks come off, and this can be an extremely vulnerable move, especially when who they are doesn't match what others believe they need to be to fit in.

TAKING A DEEPER LOOK:
ARE MODERN TEENS GROWING UP FASTER THAN THEIR PREDECESSORS?

My daughter is only fifteen, yet she acts way older. She knows about things that she's not old enough to really understand, and she wants me to treat her more like a peer. When I was her age, I didn't know half the stuff she's learning from her friends. She's growing up too fast and I don't know what to do. Is it true that teens nowadays are growing up faster compared to their predecessors?

Part of the reason parents perceive their teens as growing up too fast may be due to the onslaught of accessibility, exposure, and interactions that social media and technology afford teens. While it appears that today's teens are growing up faster, the truth is that teens are overall maturing more slowly than their predecessors, and there are some trends that show positive outcomes. For example, research has shown that teens today are less likely to engage in adult activities such as having sex and drinking, compared to previous generations. While there's no direct explanation for this change, it is believed that technology plays a role, as teens are minimizing face-to-face social interactions, taking their curiosities to the internet, and socializing and exploring behind screens.

Traditional milestones are also being met later by our teens. Studies have shown that teens are less likely to

continued >>

obtain an after-school job, drive, and date. These studies are not exclusive to gender or race; however, income was correlated with teens engaging in adult activities. Teens who come from lower-income families are more likely to engage in adult activities compared to teens who have more financial resources.

According to a survey by the Association of American Colleges and Universities, 55 percent of students in high school don't feel prepared to enter the real world, which suggests that teaching life skills such as problem-solving, planning, critical thinking, resiliency, time management, communication, empathy, and establishing boundaries and healthy relationships would be helpful.

Another aspect to consider is how some well-meaning parents hover over their teen as a means to protect or prevent failure. The problem is, if parents fear what their teen is doing or how external factors influence their teen, and therefore make efforts to control their teen's behaviors or choices, they don't allow their teen to learn these vital skills. When parents choose to let their child learn through every experience, the teen is better equipped to use these skills into the adult years.

FORGETTING "IF A BOY IS MEAN TO YOU, HE MUST LIKE YOU" & OTHER COMMON PARENTING MYTHS

"IF A BOY IS MEAN TO YOU, HE MUST LIKE YOU."

This line flows so freely from adults to teens. Why is it so easy for this message to come to life? To suggest that a boy's mean behavior is a sign of endearment has the potential to invalidate a girl's feelings and experience; additionally, it supports two other common messages: Boys aren't responsible for their actions, and boys will not be held accountable with consequences. When we re-name actions for something nicer (meanness to liking), it places responsibility on the girls to change their behaviors and excuse the behaviors of others. We want girls to feel empowered to share what's going on, including feelings. If we minimize their experience, we are indirectly telling them "It's not that big a deal."

"TEEN GIRLS ARE SASSY, SO DRAMATIC, AND TOO EMOTIONAL."

As parents, it's easy to forget that adolescence is a developmental stage in which girls are in the process of maturing. Physical and hormonal changes are happening, and hormones impact emotional regulation. Before we conclude that it's all hormones (another myth, by the way), let's consider hormones as a factor influencing potential mood swings.

The reason this myth can be troublesome is that it sends the message that teen girls are too much to handle, and if they would simply be less over-the-top, it would be easier to deal with them. Anytime we add the word "too" or "so" to emphasize a trait, there's a subtle message that says "You need to change and be less of something." Another subtle message that gets lumped in here is "You're not good enough the way you are, and you could be better." The risk here is that girls internalize these messages and determine that if they quiet their emotions, they will be more likable. As caregivers, we want the opposite—we want girls to build a strong emotional foundation that allows for free expression.

"SHE'LL GET OVER IT. IT'S JUST A PHASE."

It's fair to say that emotions aren't permanent, but ebb and flow. It's also fair to say that adolescence is a phase. However, "phase" is used loosely here to address a developmental period. When we view a behavior or emotion as a phase, we're giving ourselves permission to turn away from the experience, which creates a disconnect from our teen. We're also suggesting that the emotion or behavior isn't valid because it will be short-lived anyway. What does this translate to? It carries a new message, which is "Get over it." Turning toward the experience instead of away from it reminds teens that we have their back no matter what.

I don't think that parents are intentional in communicating these subtle messages behind the myths. Many of these myths have been long-standing in society, oftentimes handed down from generation to generation, and have become a regular part of our vocabulary. As caregivers, when we pause and take a step back to curiously dissect these myths, we find opportunities to communicate more effectively with our daughters and reinforce that their experiences are valid.

EMPOWERING GIRLS DOESN'T MEAN DISEMPOWERING BOYS

Girls continue to be given messages on how to behave as females, and these messages are in opposition to what it means to be a boy. Girls need to be sensitive and act with poise; boys need to be aggressive. Girls are caretakers; boys enter the workforce. This creates a dynamic of us-versus-them and engages socially constructed stereotypes regarding what is appropriate behavior for both girls and boys.

This brings us to gender inequality, the unequal treatment of people based on one's gender, which is largely informed by social interactions. The unequal treatment of girls can be seen in education, careers, access to health care, and family roles, to name a few scenarios—these discrepancies are all the more reason why girls need to learn empowerment.

"Empowered" has become synonymous with confidence, strength, and power—all things we want for our girls. Yet, the context in which these words have sometimes been used has the potential to disempower those around them, including boys, especially if girls are misguided regarding what it means to be empowered or aren't equipped with effective resources to feel confident doing things like setting boundaries, speaking their truth respectfully, or saying "no" if something doesn't align.

To be empowered is to make choices for oneself that are independent of outside opinion or influence. These choices are made based on the idea that the individual is the authority on their own needs and wants. Influence from others may provide an additional perspective, but does not necessarily determine the final decision. From this space, girls can take action with confidence and self-determination. Additionally, empowered girls are more likely to communicate with clear expectations and boundaries.

Empowerment doesn't stop there. In order for girls to make authentic choices, they need the appropriate skills and resources to do so. These tools include emotional intelligence, leadership, problem-solving, negotiation, creativity, and education on how to challenge and question gender norms. Unsurprisingly, research suggests that when girls are empowered, their larger communities and future generations also benefit.

Using history to inform our understanding in the here-and-now, it's important for girls to hear messages that support autonomy and decision-making, and to be able to observe male peers as teens also trying to navigate what it means to be empowered, instead of stronger, powerful, or overpowering. In doing so, a scale that was previously tipped becomes more in balance, because girls now have choices and the resources to make self-aligned decisions, becoming models for both their female and male peers.

TAKING A DEEPER LOOK: IS IT TRUE THAT SCHOOL DRESS CODES OFTEN UNFAIRLY TARGET GIRLS, ESPECIALLY GIRLS OF COLOR?

My daughter is in middle school, and looking good is really important to her. She doesn't understand her school's strict dress code. She can't always wear what's in style because she would be breaking the rules and then be ordered to wear her gym clothes. I don't want her to get in trouble, but admittedly, the dress code seems really strict. Is it true that school dress codes often unfairly target girls, especially girls of color?

The majority of research findings indicate that dress codes do in fact unfairly target girls, aligning with a sexist view. The majority of dress code policies primarily address girls' clothing, rather than the clothing of their male peers. Dress codes also tend to control what girls can and cannot wear, adding fuel to this disparity. The sexualization of girls is another defining piece of this issue, with girls subjectively judged based on how clothing fits and shamed for dress code violations. Female students who don't adhere to dress codes are often directed to change into their gym clothes, which unjustly places a target on them, causing shame and embarrassment when they have to continue with their school day dressed in clothes they did not choose to wear.

Schools will argue that the clothing of female students is a distraction to learning. Why is this problematic? First, it suggests that boys are not able to control themselves because they're focused on a girl's body instead of on the academic material. Second, it implies that because males cannot control themselves, girls need to be responsible for ensuring that their body isn't a distraction by wearing appropriate clothing. From this perspective, girls become responsible for the behaviors of boys, which is completely out of their control. Instead of focusing the strategy on talking with boys regarding healthy boundaries, schools have chosen to confront females for the "distraction" they cause, further perpetuating a cycle of shame.

To speak to race, a study by the National Women's Law Center found that African-American girls and curvier students of all races are even more impacted by school dress and grooming codes. African-American students are found to fall further behind in school due to dress-related punishments that result in them being pulled out of class or sent home. Activists recommend that schools establish dress code guidelines that support inclusivity. Such recommendations might include collaborating with students to get their input regarding policies and potential consequences for dress code violations.

STUDY PREP: YOUR POSITIVE PARENTING TIPS

- **OPEN THE DOOR TO CONVERSATIONS.** As teens question "Who am I?" against the bigger backdrop of our world, modeling honest conversations about the cultural issues present in our communities is foundational to exploring these larger issues. By holding a space without distractions for asking questions and addressing mutual emotions, parents can build opportunities to connect with their teen on concerns that are highly complicated and emotionally charged. You can start by asking, "What do you know about what's happening?"; "What are your friends talking about?"; and "How have you responded?" Let your teen lead the conversation. They will offer as much information as they're willing to discuss. Provide opportunities for your teen to ask questions of you and answer them truthfully. If you don't know the answer, it's okay to say that.

- **ENGAGE IN UNCONDITIONAL OBSERVATION.** It's hard to witness situations or experiences we don't like, agree with, or understand, such as when we observe a trend or style we don't particularly enjoy. But remember, your teen is exploring their identity. Make time to engage in their interests, curiously observing what they like, without judgment. This doesn't need to be a formal process and doesn't always have to involve questions. It can be as simple as sharing space with them. To bear witness without judgment shows your teen that you see them exactly as they are, value them, and love them unconditionally.

- **LET YOUR TEEN STRUGGLE.** Henry Ford said, "Failure is simply the opportunity to begin again, this time more intelligently." Invest time into patiently teaching your teen life skills that will support them in entering experiences independently and confidently. When you see your teen struggle, think of it as an opportunity for them to acquire a new skill, rather than a space for you to jump in to take over. Ask them open-ended questions that prompt independent thinking and problem-solving. For example, "What is one solution that will help you right now?" Allow your teen to follow through with their solution, even if you foresee an unfavorable outcome. Teens can always come back to the solution board and try again—this is why it's critical to remind teens that this concept of "failing" is actually an opportunity to use new information to choose a different solution.

- **BUST THROUGH MYTHS.** This is one of my favorites. Take a moment to list two or three parenting concepts and/or widely held beliefs that you have questioned in the past. Sit with these ideas and ask yourself, "Why have (or haven't) I questioned them?" and "What messages could this myth be sending when I say it?" Peel back the layers with whatever arises. Chances are, there's a subtle message being communicated. Next, change the statement to align with parenting values you want to prioritize. Using "It's just a phase" as an example, we can change the communication to "Your feelings are valid, and I want to support you." This new communication aligns with values centered on connection and guidance.

- **EDUCATE FOR GREATER UNDERSTANDING.** We have countless opportunities to observe the ways gender inequality exists in our society. Sit down with your teen and open a dialogue. Ask them if they know what gender inequality is and how they have observed gender inequality within their different environments. Education is key here. Teaching teens to respect all humans and to consider conventional messages about what it is to be male or female, feminine and masculine, neither or both, is an important starting point. It's essential to note that education on gender inequality is not necessarily the same as adopting new views to replace or abandon cultural, religious, or family beliefs. Education is an opportunity for further understanding of an existing concern.

KEY TAKEAWAYS

The adolescent years are packed with various and overlapping factors, but it can be difficult to acknowledge that we can't change the cultural backdrop our teens are navigating through. These larger cultural pieces inevitably influence the way teens explore the world, find their identity within different social groups, and make efforts to stand out and be unique. Teens are navigating gender inequality within different social contexts, yet the challenge continues on a macro level. How do we provide girls with the skills and resources necessary to be empowered as they approach inequalities that are so widespread? As we observe our teens navigating change, we as parents, and as a society, are called to change. For starters, we can challenge outdated ideas such as parenting myths, and approach our teens with new messages that lead us all toward greater understanding, compassion, and equality. Here are a few key takeaways from this chapter:

- Teens face big questions as they age in a cultural landscape that's packed with social issues. As they try to make sense of a sometimes chaotic world, they're asked to find their identity across many spectrums, test their identity among peers for a sense of belonging, and remove masks to showcase who they truly are.

- Gender inequality is multilayered and ever-present. Gender equality is not about tipping the scale in favor of girls receiving more than boys; it's about equal rights, where women and men are considered and valued equally. Empowerment ties into gender equality, supporting girls to learn skills to make choices for themselves and providing resources that question and challenge gender norms.

- Parenting myths that may have been carried with us from generations before are tricky, and they carry subtle underlying messages. It's important to curiously dissect parenting myths and question the inherent layers of what these myths may be communicating to our teens.

CHAPTER 2

THE DEVELOPMENT OF TEENAGE GIRLS

Most caregivers have a basic understanding of teen biology when it comes to puberty and the emotionality of teens that's readily observed in their impulsive decisions and reactive behaviors. We can see teens growing and maturing. We can observe emotional reactions. Yet, there is a gap between what we can see and what we can't. Developmental changes are also happening behind the scenes, especially when it comes to the brain.

We can't directly observe the brain, but science and research have given us opportunities to understand it is developing and how the stages of brain maturation impact the day-to-day choices, behaviors, and reactions of our teens. This chapter may feel a bit weighty with some of the technical aspects of the brain, but I can assure you that understanding these essential pieces of adolescent development will provide you with great insights and answer some of those burning "why" questions.

THIS CHAPTER WILL LOOK AT:

- The overall biology of teen development, with a focus on teenage girls

- Different theories as to why girls mature faster than boys

- The development of the teenage brain, why teens react with emotions, and why they react without thinking

- How the brain's frontal lobe functions in teens, to better understand why teens engage in risk-taking behaviors

- How the start of puberty now compares to timing in earlier years

- Whether teens are more at risk for mental health concerns than adults

Finally, we'll finish this chapter with positive parenting tools and chapter takeaways that will guide you in using findings to effectively parent your teen.

HOW GIRLS BECOME WOMEN

Adolescence—the transition from childhood to adulthood—is marked by many changes. What typically stands out for parents are the physical changes prompted by puberty; the social changes influenced by peers, social constructs, and the cultural landscape; and the emotional changes, often marked by impulsive decision-making and varying moods. Let's look at some of the specific changes teen girls encounter.

Physically, people grow more during adolescence than in any other period of their lives. An increase in height and weight is common, as are changes prompted by puberty. Hormonal changes can lead to oily skin, increased sweating, and body odor. Secondary sex characteristics also develop. For girls, this includes breast development and pubic hair growth. Menstrual periods begin occurring monthly as the body prepares for reproduction by producing more hormones. Thereafter, the body begins to release eggs from the ovaries, which means that teenage girls have the physical capability to get pregnant.

Contrary to popular belief, hormones aren't the only driving factor in adolescent behavior. Cognitive changes in the ability to think and reason are happening, too. Teens oftentimes think in very concrete, presently focused ways, yet during adolescence, they start to learn how to think in more complex ways. For example, teens learn to absorb information and think about possibilities (abstract thinking), form their own new ideas, and compare and consider different points of view. These cognitive changes look different in early (ages ten to thirteen), middle (ages fourteen to seventeen), and late adolescence (ages eighteen to twenty-one). For example, as teens progress into late adolescence, complex thinking focuses more on global concepts such as politics, justice, and their role as they enter into adulthood; whereas a teen in early adolescence is more likely focused on personal decision-making in school and at home. A child in early adolescence also starts to question authority and societal standards, whereas teens in middle adolescence tend to begin questioning and analyzing more in depth, developing their identity, forming a moral compass, and planning long-term ideas such as future goals. Teens in late adolescence are generally less focused on self-centered concepts.

Socially, teens learn to be autonomous, independently moving away from their caregivers and toward peer groups. Peer influence and relationships are hugely important, which is why you may observe your teen wanting to spend more time with their peers. This need for autonomy can feel overwhelming for both teens and parents, as it requires the family system to rethink expectations and rules that previously worked for a pre-teen child. Teens want personal ownership over areas they believe personally impact them only, yet "what is personal" is tricky, as parents want to ensure that teens are being socially responsible and making morally good decisions.

Of course, each teen matures differently. Some teens will mature sooner, while others progress later compared to teens within their same age group.

WHY GIRLS MATURE FASTER THAN BOYS

Typically, the message "girls mature faster than boys" is subjective in nature, and it isn't always followed with concrete answers as to why. Let's answer this question by looking at the research.

Girls begin puberty before their male peers, in that girls start puberty between the ages of seven and thirteen, and males start between the ages of nine and fourteen. While there's no clear-cut answer as to why, some theories have suggested that it has to do with evolution. From an evolutionary perspective, it's proposed that females matured faster so that they wouldn't choose a partner close to their same age, as males who were older were better equipped to protect and provide. While an evolutionary perspective provides a plausible reason, I believe we can say that evolution hasn't caught up with today's environment.

The brain also plays a role here. During adolescence, the brain undergoes a process that encompasses a "survival of the fittest" among neural pathways. The neural pathways that are used most often survive, and the connections that are utilized less often or are no longer needed shrink and evaporate. We will talk more about this process later, under "A Look Inside the Teenage Brain" (page 22). This process occurs between the ages of ten and twelve for girls, and between fifteen and twenty for boys, which shows that girls undergo this brain maturation process earlier. Additionally, this fine-tuning can be challenged and sometimes malfunction due to the impact of one's environment. For example, poor sleep, a lack of good nutrition, and minimal physical activity disrupt the brain's capacity to efficiently engage in this "survival of the fittest" process, and boys are more likely to be affected by these malfunctions.

Most American children spend at least 6 hours a day in a classroom, which means a large chunk of their day is spent sitting. Medical experts suggest that teens need 8 to 10 hours of sleep nightly, but the American Academy of Pediatrics has suggested that 73 percent of high school students don't get enough sleep. The takeaway here is this: Because the brain is undergoing numerous changes during this time, any opportunity to increase foundational skills around nutrition and healthy lifestyle choices is essential, while also reducing stressors within our control.

TAKING A DEEPER LOOK:
ARE GIRLS GOING THROUGH PUBERTY MUCH SOONER THAN THEY WERE BEFORE?

My daughter, who is now fourteen, started her period when she was thirteen, and started to physically develop when she was eleven. I see girls her same age who also developed closer to age eleven or twelve, and I wonder how these observable changes will impact them with the attention they are getting from their peers, especially boys. I just don't know what is true for her age, or if I should be worried about how she is feeling. Are girls going through puberty much sooner than they were before?

First, let's take a look at what puberty is and when puberty starts. Puberty is the time when a child's body develops, and these changes occur over several years. These physical changes include the growth of pubic hair, breast development, possible weight gain, the widening of hips and thighs, and increased height. On average, puberty begins between the ages of seven and thirteen in girls and starts with breast development, not menstruation. Typically, the first menstrual period starts two years after breasts begin to form.

The average age for menstruation is now thirteen, compared to sixteen or seventeen a century ago. In the U.S., breast development starts on average at age 8.8 for African-American females, while Asian, Hispanic, and white females start breast development on average between 9.3 and 9.7 years of age. While the reason as to why puberty is starting earlier for females isn't clear, researchers have theorized that increased obesity rates and exposure to pollution and hormone-disrupting chemicals may play a role.

continued >>

Starting puberty earlier than what is now considered the average age can create stress for girls. For example, girls who start menstruating earlier than their peers have been shown to be at increased risk for mental health concerns, including depression, body dissatisfaction, and anxiety-related disorders. This may be a result of self-comparison against peers who have yet to develop. Another reason for this stress may be the incompatibility between physical development and cognitive development. For example, a pre-teen who is eleven, yet physically resembles a fifteen- or sixteen-year-old, can experience social concerns such as unwanted attention. It's important to note that every girl experiences puberty differently and to acknowledge your child's unique journey within this normal maturation process.

A LOOK INSIDE THE TEENAGE BRAIN

Do you ever question why your teen is sometimes able to make rational, healthy choices that make you feel incredibly proud, yet other times they're quick to jump to conclusions, don't think things through, or are emotionally dysregulated? Teenage brain development plays a significant role in why you're seeing this.

By age six, children's brains are about 90 to 95 percent of their adult size, yet during adolescence, the brain is being "remodeled" so that it can function as an adult brain. Brain remodeling continues until about age twenty-five. The biggest change aligns with a concept of "use it or lose it," in which the brain becomes more efficient by strengthening connections. Essentially, the brain gets rid of connections that are no longer needed, while reinforcing connections that are needed. This process, called pruning, begins in the back of the brain and ends with the prefrontal cortex, part of the frontal cortex and located in the front of the brain. The prefrontal cortex is the thinking part of the brain that controls reasoning. We will talk more about the frontal cortex and its role in the next section; however, it's important to note that the frontal cortex is not fully developed until early adulthood.

Because their prefrontal cortex is still developing, teens rely on the amygdala to process information. The amygdala is the part of the brain that initiates the "fight or flight" response and manages immediate reactions, including fear. The amygdala plays a role in emotions, aggression, and impulses. This is why we see teens sometimes acting with emotions versus rational decision-making.

When you ask, "What were you thinking?" the answer might be, "I wasn't thinking." And, in part, this is true. This isn't to suggest that teens will always act emotionally or that they shouldn't be held accountable for their actions. It's to alert caregivers that the emotional part of the brain and the rational part of the brain aren't yet working like a well-balanced machine. We can expect teens at times to act impulsively, engage in risky behaviors, succumb to peer pressure, misunderstand social and emotional cues, and be less likely to pause and think about the consequences of a choice before they act or change inappropriate behaviors.

Another part of the brain, the limbic system, is responsible for primal instincts including pleasure. More clearly, the limbic system is the reward center. Findings show that there's a mismatch between this system, which matures between ages ten and twelve, and the prefrontal cortex, which isn't fully developed until age twenty-five. This explains why teens are likely to engage in reward-seeking behaviors. The pleasure and reward system are firing away, while the prefrontal cortex, which is responsible for self-control, isn't always equipped to remind teens to disengage from risky behaviors.

RULE OF THUMB: THEIR FRONTAL LOBE IS (ALMOST) ALWAYS THE CULPRIT

The frontal cortex is responsible for short-term memory storage, speech coordination, and thinking. The prefrontal cortex, which is part of the frontal cortex, regulates emotion and cognitive control. Cognitive control focuses on self-awareness and supports decision-making because it allows the mind to overrule impulses. With cognitive control, decisions are based on goals, not habits or reactions. This part of the brain is not fully developed until age twenty-five, yet the limbic system (the risk and reward system) and the amygdala (the emotional processing center) are operating at essentially full capacity in teens.

Let's tie this all together using an example of a risky behavior. Say your daughter is hanging out with her friends and they tell her to smoke a cigarette (risky behavior). She knows that smoking cigarettes isn't good for you and knows that you will be upset if she smokes. She decides to smoke anyway. Gaining the acceptance of her peers activates the limbic system. The reward of belonging wins against the less-than-average decision-making capacities of the prefrontal cortex. The prefrontal cortex doesn't stand a chance against the limbic system because it's still developing.

The still-maturing frontal cortex can't always send the message "Hey, this isn't a good idea. Think about the consequences of your choices." This is especially true when teens are with peers. Teens are highly perceptive regarding what it means to belong, and the need to be accepted becomes an automatic message that replays over and over, further reinforcing the brain's reward system.

Risk-taking looks different for every teen, and can include experimenting with alcohol, drugs, and sexual behaviors; driving too fast; or skipping school. The takeaway here is that the developing frontal cortex plays a significant role in why teens make poor choices or engage in risk-taking.

TAKING A DEEPER LOOK:
ARE TEENS MORE AT RISK FOR MENTAL HEALTH STRUGGLES THAN ADULTS?

There seem to be a lot of pressures teens are dealing with: exposure to social media, extracurricular and academic stress, and concerns about fitting in. My teen is seventeen and she's extremely hard on herself. She looks tired and stressed, she's always alone in her room, and she complains that her stomach hurts. I'm scared that something more might be going on, and depression runs in our family. With everything going on for them, are teens more at risk for mental health struggles than adults?

The answer to this question depends on which mental health concerns one is reviewing. Mental health includes mood disorders, anxiety-related disorders, behavioral disorders, substance use and abuse, eating disorders, psychosis, and personality disorders. I'm also adding suicide, thoughts of suicide, and self-harming behaviors.

The World Health Organization estimates that 10 to 20 percent of adolescents worldwide struggle with mental health issues. Risk and protective factors conversely influence mental health. Risk factors in teens can include a family history of mental illness, trauma, chronic stress, questioning sexual identity and sexual orientation (especially if family support is not provided), chaotic family and home life, substance abuse, medical conditions, developmental disabilities, poverty, and involvement with the juvenile justice system. Protective factors include strong community support, healthy relationships, family support, and a number of other components that reduce the risks associated with mental illness.

continued >>

The World Health Organization also reports that half of all mental health conditions start by fourteen years of age; however, most cases go unnoticed and untreated. In fact, globally, depression is one of the leading causes of illness and disability among adolescents. The organization also states that suicide is the fourth-leading cause of death in fifteen- to nineteen-year-olds. Among the overall adolescent population, adolescent groups most vulnerable to mental health concerns include ethnic minorities, members of the LGBTQ+ community, people in a low socioeconomic status, and those with a family history of mental illness.

As parents, how can you support your teen against mental illness? Prevention and early detection are important. Prevention is defined as any type of intervention that promotes or enhances protective factors and supports teens with emotional regulation, resiliency, healthy coping skills, and encouragement of social interactions and relationships in the community. If you suspect that your teen is struggling with mental health concerns, ask for help. Early intervention and treatment can greatly support all teens.

STUDY PREP: YOUR POSITIVE PARENTING TIPS

- **EDUCATE YOURSELF AND YOUR TEEN.** Puberty is a normal process; it can also cause a mix of excitement and confusion. It's important to educate yourself and your teen on what to expect with puberty. Have an open dialogue regarding the changes your child can expect, and provide accurate information on how the body is maturing. Use standard terms for body parts, rather than euphemisms ("vagina" versus "lady parts"). When parents show they're comfortable talking about puberty, this models development as normal, and teens are more likely to engage in the discussion.

- **FIND A BALANCE.** It's hard to stand by and watch our teens making impulsive choices. Our natural inclination is to jump in and react, which is why we need to learn to pause, step away from the situation, and re-center ourselves. Using our understanding of the still-maturing brain, we can balance praise with consequences. Teens need to know that we see the good in them, so as a parent, it's important to acknowledge times when they are making positive choices. Teens also thrive with boundaries, so when they make a bad decision, hold them accountable by integrating understanding with responsiveness. When parents approach teens with compassion, teens are more likely to engage in the discussion of what an appropriate consequence could be.

- **CREATE AN AGREEMENT—TOGETHER.** This tip comes from a foundation of understanding that teens *are* going to experiment and engage in risk-taking behaviors. This is normal. The agreement centers on you and your teen identifying what will happen when they do engage in poor decision-making. You can say, "I want you to have fun and make positive choices; I also know that sometimes you will do something you're not supposed to. I want us to talk about those moments. I agree that when you come to me, we'll talk about what happened calmly. Then, we can come up with consequences together." When teens know they can expect a collaborative talking zone, they're more likely to partake in a plan that is realistic versus punitive. Remember to praise your teen when they come to you—this will pave the way to better communication.

- **TEACH AND MODEL EMPATHY.** Empathy—the ability to share the feelings and perspectives of others—calls on us to understand others as if we were in their shoes. This approach supports the development of a teen's thinking. We can emphasize that people have different feelings, viewpoints, and circumstances, and are impacted differently by the same situation. If your teen comes to you with a story about another person, you could ask questions like, "What do you think they might have been feeling?" and "What circumstances may have led to their reaction?" These questions are open-ended and require curiosity to respond. As parents, we can serve by example by modeling empathy, too.

- **EXPLORE CONSEQUENCES AND SOLUTIONS.** You can teach your teen how to think about the short- and long-term consequences of their choices through effective problem-solving and decision-making skills. This can be done proactively or after a behavior has been carried out. Define a problem or use a real-life scenario, then list different solutions, including those with negative consequences. Next, address potential short- and long-term consequences for each solution. Choose one of these solutions, put it into action, and then evaluate the solution. Did it work? Was it met with receptivity or resistance? If a solution didn't go as expected, choose another one and try again.

- **ACKNOWLEDGE A CHANGING SYSTEM.** As teens become increasingly autonomous, make time to sit down and discuss new boundaries within the family system. Things have changed. What are new realistic expectations? When are times boundaries can be shifted? How will the family address these new boundaries? Taking a proactive approach helps prepare for transitions and supports your teen's increasing need for independence.

KEY TAKEAWAYS

To say that teen development is complex would be largely understated. Between puberty and brain development, teens are undergoing significant biological and structural changes that influence how they understand themselves and mature, moving from self-centered, concrete thinking to more global and complex thinking patterns. Understanding the stages of puberty and the developing brain provides a framework for the science behind the behaviors. Here are some key takeaways from this chapter:

- Research supports the fact that girls mature faster than boys, not only in the onset of puberty, but in how the brain is optimizing connections. Research also shows that girls are going through puberty earlier than they were before, yet there are no clear answers why.

- The teen brain is being remodeled so that it can function as an adult brain. The brain does not reach full maturity until age twenty-five. In teens, the frontal cortex is still developing and undergoing a process known as pruning. During pruning, the brain keeps often-used connections, while terminating connections that are no longer used.

- Risk-taking is a normal part of adolescence. The frontal cortex regulates emotion and cognitive control, and the fact that it's still developing largely explains why teens engage in risk-taking behaviors. Instead, the more developed parts of the brain, such as the amygdala, which emotionally processes information, and the limbic system, focused on risk and reward, play bigger roles during the teen years, which is why teens make impulsive choices and succumb to peer pressure.

CHAPTER 3

BECOMING FLUENT IN TEENAGE GIRL

Communication is key to any relationship—we need to make sure we're speaking the same language. I've heard parents exclaim, "What does that even mean?" when they recall different interactions with their daughter. Understanding the language of adolescents is a skill set that requires caregivers to keep up with the changing times and to decode information. There's a lot to keep up with, which is why I'm excited to present this chapter, dedicated to how teen girls communicate and the different dialects of social media. We'll look at:

- How teen girls communicate with parents and peers, and how teen girls express themselves emotionally

- The different components of feelings, why those feelings are important, and the benefits of emotional expression

- The language of social media, the different types of apps, and how those apps allow teens to interact with peers and a broader audience

- The intersection between performance, perfection, and comparison as it pertains to social media, and the pressures teens face to hide behind a flawless version of themselves

- Questions about meanness and inappropriate social media use

- How girls define power and navigate relationships through indirect aggression

- The risks of social media, including information on different features within popular apps

We'll close out this chapter with related tips for parents and key takeaways from the chapter.

HOW TEENAGE GIRLS COMMUNICATE

Communication is a tough arena for parents. Most caregivers acknowledge that their daughter is less likely to communicate with them now, as peers become a much bigger part of their daughter's personal bubble. It's normal for caregivers to struggle with what feels like limited communication, even with basic questions like "How was school today?" or "What do you want for dinner?" Often, questions are met with one-word responses, brief phrases, or the iconic "I don't know." It's likely that your teen will save longer communication for close friends.

That said, most teens are avid texters. Text messaging supports brief spurts of communication marked by acronyms, emojis, and GIFs. Of course, it's much easier to send "FOMO" than "fear of missing out," or the appropriate emoji to communicate that something is hysterically funny, annoying, or frustrating. Texting is convenient and provides immediate responses. From a teen's perspective, it takes way longer to call someone to confirm a meeting time than to shoot off a quick text. And it's fun—texting GIFs and emojis gives teens opportunities to express their feelings in a visual format. From this perspective, GIFs and emojis have become a universal language of understanding that doesn't require teens to share any words.

But live communication is still important. Teens at this age are starting to recognize body language and tone of voice. They're also likely to be very vocal about their opinions and speak up more. Girls will express their enjoyment of and distaste for certain situations or people and communicate in ways that others may perceive as argumentative, abrupt, or impolite. For example, as teens learn how to effectively use their voices, there may be times when they react or address concerns untactfully. It's important that parents see these viewpoints as opportunities by teens to assert their independence and integrate new(er) concepts and beliefs.

I don't want to suggest that girls are overexaggerating or overreacting in their responses. We should simply acknowledge that girls often communicate in a manner that is more emotionally expressive. For example, parents will often share about their teen, "They're so emotional," or "They're so sensitive." There's an important question here for parents to consider. Are girls truly more emotionally expressive than boys, and does the socialization of girls play a role? Findings would suggest both are true. Girls are generally more emotionally expressive compared to male peers, with traditional concepts of what's expected of females influencing communication practices. Teen girls are expected to show higher intensities of most emotions, specifically happiness, but to quiet negative emotions such as shame, guilt, anger, and sadness. Teen girls are also more likely to communicate with empathy, sympathy, and nurturance, as vulnerability and sensitivity are more socially accepted of girls.

THE IMPORTANCE OF COMMUNICATING ABOUT FEELINGS

Feelings have become synonymous with vulnerability. Many of us have been conditioned to shut them off or push them down, instead allowing rationality to be the regarded powerhouse guiding decision-making. Through this conditioning, we've steered toward negating our emotions, so when they do arise, we aren't sure what to do. To develop the necessary skills to communicate emotions requires us to regard feelings as healthy and to teach our teen girls that feelings, both comforting and discomforting, are okay.

Before girls can communicate about their feelings, however, they need to understand what their feelings are and how to talk about them. Communicating feelings is more than just identifying a feeling or having an emotional vocabulary. It also involves the ability to:

- Regulate and manage feelings

- Understand the intensity of an emotion

- Observe others' body language and facial expressions

- Connect feelings with physical sensations in the body

- Understand affect and mood congruency; that is, when an emotional reaction, including facial expressions, matches the situation or experience

All of these aspects and others influence how we share our feelings and develop healthy communication skills. These skills are associated with a host of benefits. In addition to mental health benefits, such as decreasing depression and anxiety in teens, expressing feelings in healthy ways allows teen girls to organize their thoughts and experiences, engage in effective problem-solving, and lower their physical reactions to stress.

Feelings also fuel connection. When teens have a strong emotional foundation, they're better equipped to empathize, sharing in the emotional experience of another, which also supports the ability to observe another's perspective. Feelings further encourage girls to find their internal power and confidently share their voice—two skills that contribute to self-worth and authentic interactions.

When teen girls are encouraged to feel with, and through, their feelings, they're creating foundational tools that will help them express their needs and desires effectively, ask for help, and speak up when a negative situation arises. To feel with and through an emotion asks that teen girls befriend the emotion, allowing the natural state of their feeling to be felt fully, even when the feeling doesn't feel so great. When we try to bypass emotions that we don't like or that are uncomfortable, we allow layers of unprocessed feelings to pile up. Typically, when feelings go unseen and stack too high, a breaking point occurs and emotions unravel.

TAKING A DEEPER LOOK: ARE TEENAGE GIRLS MEANER TO EACH OTHER THAN BOYS ARE?

I worry when I overhear conversations between my daughter and her friends, especially when they're talking about other girls. The names they call each other are incredibly hurtful. And some of the things they talk about sound like a game of telephone with rumors being fueled. My daughter is almost fourteen, and I want her to treat people with respect, especially fellow females. Honestly, I'm surprised by how mean she can be and how quickly she excludes other girls because her friends are doing it. I don't ever remember my son treating other boys this way when he was her age. Are teenage girls meaner to each other than boys are?

The research is mixed. Some studies suggest that gender differences exist within forms of indirect aggression, social aggression, and relational aggression, with girls being more aggressive, yet this gender difference is relatively small. In a study from the University of Georgia, findings suggested that boys are meaner than girls, through both indirect and physical forms of aggression. This same study also found that relational and physical aggression for both genders

continued >>

is highest during middle school—sixth through eighth grades—and then declines throughout high school.

I will use indirect aggression to encompass relational and social aggression here, as studies have shown that they share more similarities than differences. Indirect aggression includes behaviors that create harm through body language and verbal language. Indirect aggression is not physical in nature; rather, it can include dirty looks, spreading rumors, attacking someone's social status, excluding someone, sharing secrets discussed in confidence, breaking trust, and encouraging peers to dislike or turn against another person.

We know that fitting in is a top priority among adolescents, and the ways in which girls behave to fit in are unique. For girls, popularity is correlated with power, and often, girls use being mean as a way to gain social status in a group. Popular girls are more likely to be mean, whereas girls with a lower position in a group are likely to use kindness as a means to gain status. As caregivers, it's helpful to remember that girls aren't being mean just to be mean. They're engaging in not-so-nice behaviors as a tool to fit in and gain social status among their female peers. It's still not right, but at least it shines a light on the reason for the behavior—it all comes back to the pressure to fit in.

UNDERSTANDING THE DIFFERENT SOCIAL MEDIA DIALECTS

Teens seem to effortlessly speak the language of social media, while most parents scramble to keep up with a dialect that continues to change and expand. Like any language we learn, we need to start with basic terminology. Here, social media basics will address the different forms of social media and the types of interactions they facilitate among teens.

The categories of social media are vast and ever-changing. They include social networking, photo and video sharing, blogging, and community-building platforms. Social networking is likely the most familiar to caregivers; it allows teens to stay connected and interact with one another. Through these sites, teens can upload and share pictures and videos; tag their peers; share content by topic or theme with hashtags (#); react to content with a "like," "love," or "dislike"; share and re-share posts; and private-message one another.

Photo and video sharing are exactly what they imply. Teens can post and comment on photos and videos. Some sites known as bookmarking sites allow teens to save and organize links from a variety of online resources. Through bookmarking sites, teens can create vision boards of favorite quotes, wish lists, clothing styles, or music interests.

Social media also allows for connection within specific communities. Community-building platforms provide discussions among a group of people where a specific question or topic can be posted, and readers can respond with their own ideas, experiences, and opinions. Teens don't have to write a response to participate; they can simply read the content.

Blogging, when a person shares written material about different topics or experiences with readers, provides opportunities to share content and opens the door for further discussion among those who have read the blog. Blog content is often provided on a consistent basis. Once the blog is posted by the writer, readers can comment on what the individual has written via a comment section. In turn, the writer and other viewers of the blog can respond to the readers' comments.

Other common social media terms include "memes," "GIFs," "vlogging," and "group chats." Memes can include any form of content, be it a video, written text, or image with wording that is copied and shared. Memes are typically humorous and spread rapidly. They can include content about beliefs, stories, or phrases. GIFs are videos that can be shared, that repeat on a loop without the recipient needing to press play. Essentially, teens (or anyone) can use GIFs to express their thoughts or feelings, just like they would when using an emoji. Vlogging is similar to blogging, yet the shared content is provided in video form. Vlogs can cover an array of content and themes including tutorials, travel, music, and educational materials. A group chat is a common messaging thread, similar to text messaging, shared among a group of people.

THE PRESSURES TO PERFORM ON SOCIAL MEDIA

Performance and perfection tie together on social media, interweaving in a way that places immense pressure on teens. Research supports this concern, noting that 37 percent of teens feel pressured to receive "likes" from viewers, and 43 percent feel pressured to keep up a certain appearance online. Considering how much time teens spend on social media, understanding how and why teens engage as they do is essential to understanding them and what drives them. It's also important that parents keep up with social media trends and be aware of potential dangers.

At a time when teens are looking to fit in, social media culture fuels this inherent desire through what I term "online validation." Online validation is the acceptance teens feel when viewers engage positively with their shared content. The more positive validation they receive, the more teens feel a sense of being "good enough," and the more compelling the cycle to post appealing content appears. When teens receive a "like" on social media, the brain produces dopamine, a "feel-good" neurotransmitter associated with pleasure. Think about it. How often have you observed your teen instantly engaging with their phone the second a notification goes off? They want to see how others have responded.

Teens feel the need to post engaging content to receive online validation. Engaging content appeals to viewers and draws attention to the individual posting. Teens can receive immediate feedback that implies, "We like you, you're good enough." To boost their success rate, teens find numerous ways to put the best versions of themselves online. Filters and photo editing allow teens to change the way they look, creating flawless photos to share. Apps have even been created allowing teens to change their facial features, whether it's a smaller nose or fuller lips. Numerous tutorials also share tips with teens on how to take photos that are both attractive and appealing. It's easy to see the problem with this, right?

Indeed, social media has created a culture that supports putting only the best aspects of our life into the public eye. Teens can create a false narrative of "everything is perfect," leaving the sometimes-messy realities of life behind a screen and fueling unhealthy comparisons. If teens constantly see idealized versions of others' lives online, it's invariably going to make them feel less-than, as though their life is lacking. In a study of older adolescents, those who engaged with social media passively, merely looking at others' photos, expressed a decrease in life satisfaction, compared to peers who use social media to post content or interact with others. Indeed, interacting to connect or stay in contact with others is likely to provide better results compared to someone who is posting just to stay relevant or looking for likes to validate their sense of self.

TAKING A DEEPER LOOK:
ARE TEENS USING CERTAIN SOCIAL MEDIA APPS TO SEND INAPPROPRIATE CONTENT?

My daughter is glued to her phone. She's constantly on platforms that I'm not familiar with. I don't know what she's viewing or what she shares. When I peek over her shoulder or ask for her phone, she becomes very secretive. Like most parents I know, there's a constant worry that social media is an avenue for cyberbullying, adults preying on underaged kids, or sharing or asking for inappropriate pictures. Are teens using certain social media apps to send inappropriate content?

Social media allows teens to learn from and share content, connect with larger communities, sustain relationships, and find fun. Yet, there's this very large, abstract gray area behind the screen that is unknown to many caregivers. Most parents understand the bigger risks associated with social media. Still, many parents aren't clear on how the smaller features within these apps work, such as video chat options, secret chat rooms, live streaming, location tracking, and settings that allow a profile to remain public or private.

One strategy that has been marketed to teens is the "disappearing" photo or video. While most teens lean toward sending silly videos and pictures, the false premise around supposedly temporary photos (keep in mind, anyone can take a screenshot of a temporary photo) can increase the likelihood of teens sharing provocative photos or engaging in sexting—exchanging, sending, or receiving messages or visuals of a sexual nature. Another strategy targets a teen's ability to remain anonymous. For example, one social platform allows teens to anonymously post what's on their minds, accompanied by a picture. The risk here is exposure to, and the sharing of, inappropriate content.

Self-education on the different social media apps your teen uses and how they work is a great start. The internet can provide substantial information regarding what the different apps entail and how to reduce social media risks by complying with age requirements or knowing how to turn off specific features like location tracking. Engaging with your teen in an open dialogue about the risks and benefits of social media is also key. Here are a few tips for engaging them:

- Start the conversation from a young age.
- Ask your teen regularly what websites and apps they are using (don't assume).
- Address the need for personal information to remain private online.
- Take a collaborative approach to setting realistic bound-aries around social media use.

STUDY PREP: YOUR POSITIVE PARENTING TIPS

- **MEET YOUR TEEN WHERE THEY'RE AT.** While parents would prefer that their teen talk to them directly and face-to-face, a teen would argue that any form of commu-nication is sufficient. Knowing that teens use indirect forms of communication, it can actually be helpful to meet your teen with their preferred style of communication, including via text messages or private messages on social media. While this may not be ideal to you, you're likely to get a response from your teen—and maybe even a laugh. This isn't to replace direct forms of communication, nor am I suggesting that conversations around safety or risk should be handled behind a screen. Just consider that sometimes a text message exchange can make for easy and painless communication.

- **HELP THEM UNDERSTAND THEIR BODY'S RESPONSES.** When your teen comes to you upset and looking for help, you can encourage them to sit with their uncomfortable feelings. You might ask, "Where do you feel the anger in your body?" or "What does this feeling of anxiety feel like in your body?" It's okay to provide descriptors such as sharp, dull, throbbing, sweaty, heavy, etc. You'll find that the more your teen is feeling with the emotion physically, the more likely the feeling will subside. I suggest starting this practice with emotions that are felt at a lower intensity, such as nervousness that feels like a 3 on a scale of 1 to 10, with 10 being the highest intensity. During this practice, encourage your teen to pay attention to their breath and think about the sensations in their body without judgment. You know your teen best. Consider when it's appropriate to suggest this practice, and when they just need some space.

- **HELP THEM REFLECT ON AGGRESSION AND ITS CONSEQUENCES.** Teen girls aren't likely to associate their style of interactions with definitive terms such as "indirect aggression." Caregivers can provide moments of self-reflection to address how girls interact with one another. Providing a definition for indirect aggression and exploring how females assert and gain social status is key. Ask closed-ended questions to start, such as, "Have you ever been excluded by a group?" or "Have you ever started or fueled rumors?" You can follow these with open-ended questions, including "What was it like to experience that exclusion?" or "How do you think someone might feel if they are the one being talked about?"

- **DISCUSS PERFECTION VERSUS AUTHENTICITY.** Start a conversation about your teen's experience with social media. Bring up the pressures to perform on social media and whether they notice an expectation to project perfection over authenticity. Discuss with your teen how the majority of people share the best versions of themselves online, and ask your teen about their own experience with how they represent themselves. Have they shared accurate portrayals or false representations of who they are? Did one version feel better than the other? If so, how and why? Address aspects such as photo-editing tools and filters, and how it's extremely brave for them to show up as who they really are. Teens need to hear that everyone has aspects about themselves that they wish to hide or change, and that perfection is an unobtainable expectation—for anybody.

- **WORK TOGETHER TO ESTABLISH SOCIAL MEDIA EXPECTATIONS.** Not only is it helpful to do your own research on social media, including the specific platforms your teen uses and how they can safely engage on different apps, it's also essential to talk with your teen regarding the expectations around social media, including:
  - What apps are they allowed to use?
  - What features on these apps are they allowed to use?
  - What information are they allowed to share and not share?
  - What expectations do they have for themselves and their interactions with others?
  - What can happen if they engage in ways that pose safety concerns?
  - How can they use social media responsibly?

KEY TAKEAWAYS

If this chapter has taught us anything, it's that communication is supported by an emotional menu that encompasses more than just tone of voice or physical sensations in the body, and the ways in which teen girls communicate are facilitated through different avenues. These avenues include face-to-face interactions (even through sometimes limited verbal responses with caregivers and other adults), indirect communication with peers, and social media platforms that enable teens to interact, share, and observe in many different ways. Here are other key takeaways from this chapter:

- In the same way that feelings are multilayered, communication is multifaceted. Communication is much more than just the sharing of words, just as the expression of feelings is more than simply identifying an emotion. Teen girls are more emotionally expressive compared to male peers, with gender norms and socialization playing a role. Research supports the fact that teen girls are often discouraged from expressing their discomforting emotions.

- Feelings fuel connection, and when teen girls are encouraged to feel with and through emotions, instead of pushing down or distracting from them, they create foundational skills to integrate and address feelings with greater ease and confidence.

- Teens are inundated with pressure to perform on social media. Performance is influenced by online validation, the creation of noteworthy content, perfectionistic attitudes for posting flawless pictures, and comparison themes perpetuated by others posting idealized versions of themselves. Brain chemistry also stimulates the desire to perform in this area with dopamine, a "feel-good" neurotransmitter associated with pleasure.

- Social media creates a huge learning curve for caregivers, as social media apps are constantly changing in their popularity among teens. Social media involves its own language and requires its own instruction manual to comprehend the differences between social networking, photo and video sharing, blogging, and community-building platforms, and to reduce the potential risks associated with social media. Parents are encouraged to learn about the different platforms and their risks, and to talk to their teens about those risks in order to help prevent personal danger or damage to reputation. A simple internet search for "what do I need to know about social media" is a good place to start.

CHAPTER 4

THE SOCIAL LIFE OF TEENAGE GIRLS

Navigating relationships can be tough, even for adults. They require us to be connected and to practice communication and the art of vulnerability. Relationships are best supported by patience and understanding, both for ourselves and others. Good relationships can be extremely rewarding, especially when we find a perfect match in a friend or romantic partner. This chapter is all about relationships, including the benefits of strong relationships and how relationships support teen development. We'll address:

- Why it's important for teens to have strong friendships, and how friendships serve as an extension of the family unit

- The benefits associated with having a diverse friend group, including what diversity means and how teens identify and integrate their interactions with these different groups

- The significance of dating and romantic relationships, including how dating is a healthy part of teen development, myths associated with romantic relationships, and what it means to be a healthy romantic partner

- How being a good friend is similar to being a good partner

- Answers to questions about what to do if you suspect your daughter's friend is a bad influence, and how to deal if you don't like who your teen is dating

As always, we'll end the chapter with helpful parenting tips to support your teen in effectively exploring relationships as they continue to form their own identity.

THE IMPORTANCE OF STRONG FRIENDSHIPS

Relationships have the capacity to harness connections and expand our sense of belonging; in fact, they are a cornerstone of being human. As teens move away from the family system during adolescence and explore their independence, having meaningful relationships of all types and with all genders is foundational for positive development.

Teens find their fit among peers, and it's natural for them to engage with different people and groups. Not all interactions will result in a solid friendship. Some peers become acquaintances, where exchanges remain superficial; other friendships blossom into a best friend or a close-knit circle of friends. Each relationship fills different needs, and close relationships provide affiliation and acceptance. When teens focus on sustaining and maintaining strong bonds, their mental health improves, including their sense of self-worth and confidence. Strong friendships also correlate with future mental health. Studies have shown that teens who have close friendships during adolescence demonstrate decreased symptoms of anxiety and depression as adults, compared to teens who have a larger friend group but lack close connections. The takeaway here is that having a lot of friends isn't necessarily better than having a few strong friendships with a deep sense of connection.

Friendships also support a stronger immune system, emotional regulation, trust for others, and a stronger sense of overall happiness. In many ways, friendships are an extension of the individual teen, as well as of the family unit. As teens begin to socialize more with peers, they also share and confide more in them; friends become a sounding board for future interactions, decision-making, and problem-solving. This extension serves as a parallel dynamic to the family unit. In just the same way a teen wants to be accepted by their caregivers and family, teens want their friends to like them unconditionally, exactly as they are. Strong connections provide this acceptance that teens are looking for.

Similarly, this expansion from home to friends allows teens to explore friends who are both alike and different from themselves. When teens have friends who are unique and prioritize different values, they encounter new experiences to vicariously learn from these peers, engage in interests that they may not otherwise explore, and find direct and indirect opportunities for perspective-taking and empathy. For example, if your daughter is shy, yet her friend is outgoing, it's likely that your teen will discover more moments to practice socializing and increased chances to meet new people. If, on the other hand, your teen is the outgoing friend to a shy teen, this provides opportunities for your teen to support their friend and practice patience as their friend slowly warms up to new people.

Friendships also provide support through shared experiences, especially when teens face tough situations, such as parents divorcing or losing a friendship. Talking to caregivers isn't necessarily the first go-to for teens—they need their peers to relate. Friends who can say, "I know what that's like," or "I've experienced that, too," provide a safe space to address some of life's not-so-easy transitions.

A DIVERSE FRIEND GROUP IS ALSO KEY

Diversity means variety, but it extends beyond racial, ethnic, and gender differences. Diversity also includes gender identity, sexual orientation, physical and intellectual abilities, political views, age, religion, social standing, and more. Embracing diversity is about respecting and valuing the differences of others, and recognizing that each of us is uniquely different.

As most teens mature, they are largely exposed to cultural practices and belief systems that are specific to their own family of origin and community. This isn't to suggest that interaction with diverse individuals hasn't happened; it's to remind us that how we grow up and interact with others can determine how much exposure we've had to different cultures. Having a diverse friend group allows teens to observe practices and beliefs different from their own, creating a foundation for more open-mindedness, acceptance, perspective-taking, and inclusivity.

Interactions with others naturally provide a foundation for personal development, as every experience offers an opportunity for growth. Teens are constantly learning from those around them, and when they have interactions with different populations, they integrate these experiences to further identify who they are within the larger community and world. Additionally, diversity supports teen girls in curiously exploring the world through the experience of others, so as they solidify their own identity, they also learn about how the greater cultural landscape affects other people.

It's generally easier for girls to engage with others who they perceive as similar to themselves. Yet, when girls focus on similarities they have with other individuals from different groups, they're more likely to engage in situations that encourage them to step out of what feels familiar. This stepping-out has great benefits for self-confidence. Research has identified that adolescents with more self-confidence are more likely to step in and stand up for fellow peers who are being bullied. Children with diverse friends are also found to show increased levels of resiliency and greater leadership potential.

One final note: Studies have indicated that a diverse school environment doesn't necessarily provide opportunities for diverse friendships, so how can caregivers help? One strategy is to encourage teens to foster positive attitudes about meeting individuals who are different from themselves. This helps reduce negative stereotypes and increases their comfort and willingness to step into new interactions. You can find additional ways to embrace diversity in the Study Prep section at the end of this chapter (page 57).

TAKING A DEEPER LOOK: I'VE HEARD THAT ONE OF MY DAUGHTER'S FRIENDS IS A BAD INFLUENCE. WHAT SHOULD I DO?

I've heard that one of my daughter's friends is a bad influence. Other parents have warned me, telling me that she's bad news. Supposedly, this friend gets in trouble a lot, doesn't care about her grades, and vapes on occasion. I have done my best to keep their interactions very limited or have them spend time at our house, but my daughter keeps asking to hang out with her outside the house. I know that if I let her go to a public space, I have limited control over what happens. What should I do?

I don't recommend telling your teen to cut this friend out, as you'll likely be met with resistance. Hearing details from other parents is just one piece of the information pie that will influence how you move forward. What are your direct observations of this friend? What information do you have to support or negate the claims from other parents? There's a reason your teen is drawn to this friend. Have you asked your teen why they enjoy hanging out with them? It can be extremely enlightening to ask your teen for their perspective.

continued >>

If the information from other parents is false, this makes your decision easier. If, though, this friend is truly a bad influence, communicate your concerns. The goal of this communication isn't to convince your teen that their friend is bad—that's a direct road to conflict. The goal is to express your concerns, review household expectations, and address how you can hold one another accountable. Accountability can look something like, "I trust that you can make good choices when you're with your friends, and I will do my best to stand in the background without judgment." Unless you observe safety concerns or your teen is directly breaking household expectations, it's important to remain patient and allow your teen to navigate their way through this friendship. Chances are, they'll eventually identify for themselves that this friend may not be the best influence.

If your teen is unwilling to communicate directly with you, stick to open-ended questions that focus on other healthy friendships, instead of questions that target this specific friend. Also, if you find your teen questioning their relationship with this friend, use it as an opportunity to listen without judgment and support your teen to make self-directed choices on how to address what's happening.

DATING IS HEALTHY (AND NOT ALWAYS JUST ABOUT SEX)

The topic of dating is a challenging one for caregivers. Much of what we hear about teen dating is slightly misguided. Dating myths perpetuate parenting fears, which doesn't help ease these worries. A few that come to mind include that "dating leads to sex," "teens don't know what true love is," and "if I have 'the talk' with my teen, they'll think having sex is okay." Romance and dating are a very normal part of adolescence. Having accurate information on what to expect and why it's important for teens to explore healthy dating relationships can help relax some of your parenting fears.

Teens learn through relationships, and like any relationship, romantic relationships require a set of skills. Dating builds relationship skills such as effective communication, problem-solving, demonstrating compassion and kindness, setting boundaries, and perspective-taking. Dating additionally asks teens to put themselves out there, whether it's to experience a first date or to acknowledge that they have a crush on someone. This vulnerability isn't easy, as it leaves teens open to the potential for hurt feelings and rejection. However, while rejection is often painful, it can also be beneficial. Rejection increases patience, allows different options to be explored, creates opportunities for change, and helps provide perspective. These benefits, however, are most supportive to a teen's growth when the feelings associated with the rejection are addressed and explored.

Also significant is how relationships encourage teens to learn their own interaction style in relation to a partner and the expectations they have of a romantic partner. For example, some teens want to spend all of their time with their partner, while others seek more of a balance between connection and independence. In the years I've worked with teens, this has been a challenging arena for them. Teens often have an idealized version of what dating looks like—a fairy tale supported by movies and other forms of media. It takes time to figure out that real-life relationships are very different. Teens are learning as they go, figuring out what feels right for them, in addition to navigating these newer skills against a developing brain that is still learning impulse control. Without these dating experiences, teens wouldn't have the space to develop the skills that help define and fine-tune who they are as a partner and what they expect of others romantically.

Contrary to popular belief, having conversations with one's teen regarding sex has been correlated with teens waiting longer to engage in sexual intercourse and the likelihood that birth control will be utilized. It's also important for conversations to move beyond just sexual intercourse and include discussions around consent and enthusiastic consent (which we'll discuss), dating safety, and peer pressure. While these are tricky discussions for both teens and caregivers, addressing these aspects will create more trust and openness between you and your teen when it comes to dating.

BEING A GOOD FRIEND ISN'T UNLIKE BEING A GOOD GIRLFRIEND

Every home has different rules about dating, and the most common question I hear is "When should I allow my teen to start dating?" There's no hard rule on a specific age, yet I do recommend that conversations about romantic relationships begin before your teen has their first romantic partner. As caregivers, it's easy to forget that romantic relationships are a new territory for teens. Romance brings forth big moments for teens including crushes, a first kiss, potential heartbreak, and possible sexual interactions, and girls need support to understand what a healthy relationship entails.

Teen girls are likely to feel more secure in their blueprint for how to be a good friend than in their ability to be a good romantic partner, partly because they've had more practice with friendships, and partly because teens often attach a different value to romantic relationships. With this latter idea, vulnerability plays a role, as it clouds over a basic truth; while romantic relationships carry a different dynamic compared to friendships, at the core of both types of relationships is an interaction between two people. Teens need to be reminded that relationships, friendly or romantic, require interactions based on foundational values and skills such as trust, respect, honesty, communication, and a balance of power, to name a few. The same qualities and values they hold for friendships can translate to relationships with romantic partners.

When teens have a healthy blueprint for relationships through both direct and indirect experiences and observations, they are more likely to apply these blueprints to friendships and romantic partners. This especially applies to the immediate relationships in the home environment. So, what happens when a healthy blueprint hasn't been provided? Risks can include engaging in relationships that lack positive communication skills, poor problem-solving, poor conflict management, and negating one's own identity and needs. On the extreme end of the spectrum lies the risk of engaging in an abusive relationship. Abuse takes different forms, including physical, verbal, emotional, and sexual, and an abusive relationship increases the likelihood of poor self-esteem, symptoms of depression and anxiety, and continued engagement in at-risk behaviors.

TAKING A DEEPER LOOK:
WHAT SHOULD I DO IF I DON'T LIKE WHO MY DAUGHTER IS DATING?

My daughter is sixteen and she's been dating someone new for about a month. She was honest with us from the beginning, which has been great. But I don't like who she's dating. I don't want to tell her that she can't date them, yet there's a part of me that secretly hopes their relationship doesn't work out. It's really hard being around them, and I sort of cringe whenever she talks about them. I'm trying to be supportive, yet it's really tough being inauthentic. What's the best approach?

Realistically, you're not always going to like who your daughter chooses to date. Ask yourself a few questions

continued >>

to self-reflect. What is it that you don't like about them? Are these unlikable qualities aspects that you personally don't want for your teen? If so, dig deeper as to why. How do you really feel about your daughter dating? While these questions seem straightforward, it's important to get real with ourselves about what's influencing our concern. Oftentimes, there's more to uncover.

Once you've explored these questions and established that no safety concerns exist, remember that this relationship is significant to your daughter and that she wants you to be supportive. Support doesn't equal agreement. It does, however, mean that when she comes to you to talk about her relationship, you're doing your best to listen without judgment and allowing her to make choices that make sense for her. As the parent, you should engage as a listener and do your best to steer clear of giving unsolicited advice. Teens sometimes read this kind of advice as control or forcing a specific action. This can signal your teen to retract and not share further.

Teens are great at picking up on how their caregivers feel, even when we think we're hiding our true emotions. This intuition is especially on point when distress is part of the equation. When teens pick up that we don't like something or someone that is important to them, they'll pull away. Pulling away looks different for every teen, yet a common disconnecting tactic for them is to stop talking about the thing or person we don't like. We want our teens to view us as a supportive ally, and we want them to communicate honestly.

STUDY PREP: YOUR POSITIVE PARENTING TIPS

- **ENGAGE THEIR CIRCLE.** I cannot stress enough how critical it is for parents to know their teen's friends and dating interests. It's also good to get to know the caregivers of these peers. This doesn't need to be a formal sit-down. It could involve asking your teen about these individuals or offering to drive the teens to their next outing. It's amazing how much information you can gather simply by being a quiet observer. Other avenues include inviting their peers over for dinner, encouraging them to hang out at your house, and, when peers come over, asking them questions. This isn't an interrogation; it's questioning with curiosity.

- **SUPPORT DIVERSITY WITH CREATIVE SOLUTIONS.** School doesn't always lead to diverse friendships. To support diversity, encourage your teen to join a school club that is different from what they know or are used to. Heritage months and diversity months, when unique groups are recognized, also create opportunities to learn about different cultures and their histories. Attending different festivals or joining classes that highlight different cultural practices such as music or dance are also great options. Media can also provide learning opportunities through documentaries and shows.

- **ASK YOURSELF, "WHAT'S UNDER THE SURFACE?"** A big part of parenting is self-reflection and identifying our own process as it pertains to certain situations. For example, caregivers typically have responses to their teen starting to date. When an unsettling situation arises, or you're having a reaction to an experience in front of you, take 5 to 10 minutes to answer some of these questions:

- What is it that I'm feeling right now?
- What thoughts are coming up for me?
- What is it about this situation that makes me uneasy or uncomfortable?
- How can I be most responsive, not reactive?
- How can I balance my teen's need for autonomy with my intention of wanting to be effective in my support?

When we take time to listen to our inner workings, we're likely to identify that there's more going on than what's on the surface, and we give ourselves an opportunity to engage more fully with our teen because we are more responsive to their need.

- **CREATE TEMPLATES FOR RELATIONSHIPS.** Sit down with your teen and create a template that addresses how they want to behave in relationships, friendly or romantic, and their expectations of the other person. Questions that can help you brainstorm include:
  - What are my values and what's important to me in a relationship?
  - How do I expect others to treat me?
  - What are deal-breakers or things that will lead me to end the relationship?
  - What do I expect of myself? Be specific. For example, trust is a great value, but what does trust look like with words and in behaviors? How would I know that someone is being trustworthy? What does it *not* look like?

- **EXPAND ON "THE TALK."** It's ideal to have an initial conversation about safe sex, boundaries, enthusiastic consent, and birth control methods with your teen prior to their first romantic relationship. It's crucial that conversations are had both in confidence and with confidence. It's okay to admit that it's an awkward discussion for both of you, but if your teen suspects that you're uneasy or wishy-washy, they may pull back from these topics. Address what sex is and different forms of birth control. Stress what consent is and isn't, and why it's necessary. Address how your teen can create boundaries around romantic relationships and what to do if they feel uncomfortable in any way.

KEY TAKEAWAYS

For teens, relationships outside the home become reliable sources for connectedness and belonging. Strong friendships and engagement with diverse individuals are foundational and provide many benefits to girls. Romantic relationships are also fundamental, and teens need support in learning how to be a good partner. Helpful reminders that dating relationships require a similar skill set to friendships can help ease dating firsts for girls and let them recognize that they already have a general skill set on how to interact in relationships. Here are a few other takeaways from this chapter:

- Relationships are an area for learning and growth for teens. Within these different relationships, teens are asking, "Who am I in the context of these relationships?" Through these relationships, teens hone skills such as communication and problem-solving, and use the experiences of others to observe how the world operates—this further solidifies belief systems and how they think, and provides templates for how to interact with others.

- Caregivers will not always like who their teen is friends with or dates. It's important for loved ones to remember that teens are choosing these individuals; therefore, it's not recommended to jump in and restrict these interactions right away. Unless safety concerns exist or your daughter is making risky decisions that are outside healthy development, the best course of action is to reserve judgment and remember that teens are learning through these different relationships.

- Romantic relationships and dating are both healthy and normal parts of the adolescent stage. It's important to remember that dating relationships are new to teens, and that they're experiencing many firsts that can exacerbate feelings of vulnerability. This is also a tough arena for caregivers, but dating is not always about sex. Having conversations about dating, boundaries, safety practices, and methods of protection is also key.

CHAPTER 5

DISCUSSING BODY IMAGE & BULLYING WITH TEENAGE GIRLS

Body image and bullying are complex topics, and both have recently received widespread attention. Much of the awareness has come as a result of increased knowledge for how these aspects affect our youth and the larger community. We have progressed forward in many ways; however, body image and bullying are still at the forefront of the challenges that teens face.

IN THIS CHAPTER, WE'LL LOOK AT:

- The warning signs to determine if your teen is being bullied or bullying others, and parenting tips to help support you either way

- Online bullying, how dynamics shift when bullying enters the chatroom, and how it affects its targets

- What body image is, struggles teens face with body-image issues, and how to help your daughter who may or may not be vocal about these challenges

- Newer ways to approach beauty standards, focusing on character and personality versus external validation.

- Answers to questions about cutting and eating disorders

    To end, we'll offer parenting tips specific to these topics.

ARE THEY BEING BULLIED OR
ARE THEY THE BULLY?

We now understand how tragic bullying can be. We've seen this with school shootings, where perpetrators of school violence have expressed, through evidence left behind, their own experiences of severe bullying. We also now know that those being bullied are more likely to have thoughts of suicide and follow through with committing suicide. While these responses lie at the extreme end of the spectrum, each person experiences bullying differently, and at its root, it is a painful and damaging experience.

The warning signs for bullying aren't always apparent, yet red flags include:

- Observable changes in behaviors or a change in academics. For example, have you seen a decline in your teen's grades, or have they suddenly expressed that they don't want to go to school anymore?

- Sleep disturbances, including nightmares, increased sleeping, and difficulties falling asleep.

- Changes in eating habits, including a loss of appetite or infrequent eating, and overeating that may or may not cause weight gain.

- Physical symptoms such as headaches, stomachaches, nausea, or any other reports of illness.

- Mental health concerns including anxious mood, sadness or depression, low self-esteem, mistrust of others, and social withdrawal.

- Observable bruises or injuries on your teen, damaged possessions, or lost items. These can indicate that something bigger is happening at school.

Parents are more apt to ask questions to assess bullying from the perspective of the victim, but what happens when your teen is the one doing the bullying? First, it's important to know what to look for. Teens who engage in bullying typically:

- Have frequent interactions with school personnel or administrators to address behavioral concerns or aggressive behaviors such as physical fighting or verbal altercations with peers.

- Move in "peer packs" or with friends who also bully or instigate behaviors of aggression.

- Demonstrate difficulty taking responsibility for their actions, show a lack of remorse, and/or come home with new items that have suspicious explanations.

- Place a high value on popularity and reputation.

What can you do if your teen is bullying others? It's critical to step in with accountability and understanding. To clarify, understanding is not normalizing or excusing the behaviors. It is acknowledging that bullying is about power and control and runs deeper than the bullying behaviors we observe. Oftentimes, those who bully face their own struggles. This requires that caregivers take a balanced approach that is psychoeducational in nature and opens a dialogue of curiosity. Psychoeducation involves providing your teen with information on what bullying is, the different forms of bullying, how bullying impacts victims, and why teens bully. Curiosity ties into this latter piece—asking open-ended questions can help your teen start thinking about what leads them to bully others. Specific questions to ask can be found on page 74.

WHEN BULLYING ENTERS
THE CHATROOM

Online bullying, or cyberbullying, is a form of bullying and harassment that occurs through the use of digital devices such as tablets, computers, and cell phones. Through these devices, teens can utilize text messages, social media platforms, online gaming communities, emails, photos, and different forums to send, post, share, and comment in ways that are negative, harmful, and shaming to the targeted person.

The humiliation that comes with online bullying is distinctive in many ways. Content posted publicly carries the consequence of staining an individual's reputation. This stain also affects the person posting the negative information. Posts essentially become archived information that remains accessible both in current time and in the future, and show a timeline of people's views, actions, and behaviors. For the victim, social platforms allow for repetitive bullying that feels never-ending unless content is removed. This public accessibility can also feel insurmountable, as content can reach a broader audience and spread quickly. What's more, the digital world doesn't sleep—it runs 24 hours a day, 7 days a week, so there's no break from the flood of online information. Teens already feel socially overwhelmed with the pressures to fit in; for information to be broadcast so publicly violates one's sense of self.

While some posts are public, anonymity also plagues victims of cyberbullying. Social media and online forums allow people to utilize screen names, hiding the actual identity of the aggressor. Anonymity allows for more severe bullying behaviors, as the bully may feel invincible behind a screen. If a bully cannot be named, those being bullied are without protection, and consequences cannot be addressed.

Online bullying leaves those targeted vulnerable in many ways, and often, teens being cyberbullied don't share that it's happening. As a parent, please don't take this personally.

Cyberbullying can feel overwhelming, embarrassing, and confusing to those on the receiving end, yet there are warning signs to look for. These signs may include:

- A change in your teen's demeanor around technology, shifting from frequent to less frequent use, or complete withdrawal from technology.

- Disconnecting from friends.

- Changes in mood, including sadness, anger, or anxious behaviors.

- Secretive behaviors when it comes to online interactions.

Having open conversations with your teen about any observed changes is key to addressing, resolving, and preventing cyberbullying and any feelings of helplessness or shame.

TAKING A DEEPER LOOK: I'VE HEARD THAT TEENS WHO ARE BULLIED RESORT TO CUTTING. WHAT IS THAT, AND SHOULD I BE WORRIED?

My teen, who is fourteen, has been on the receiving end of bullying. I fear that the bullying will affect more than just her self-worth. She appears to be sad more often than not and doesn't know how to assert herself when peers pick on her. I know that she's struggling with self-confidence, and I worry that her feelings will turn into something bigger like depression. I've also been reading a lot online about what can happen when teens are being bullied and the outcomes make me extremely concerned. I've heard that teens who are bullied resort to cutting. What is that, and should I be worried?

continued >>

Cutting can be a fear-inducing topic for parents—for good reason—yet when cutting is understood, it's much easier to navigate this behavior with your teen. Cutting is a form of self-injury or self-harm in which one purposely chooses to use a sharp object or other means, such as their fingernails, to cut or scratch an area of the body. Cutting can occur as a one-time incident or become a recurring pattern of behavior that requires more serious intervention. Warning signs may include:

- Wearing long sleeves or pants, even in warm temperatures.
- Scars or cuts, sometimes in patterns.
- Expressions of helplessness or worthlessness.
- Frequent reports of injury.
- The presence of sharp objects.

Why do teens engage in cutting behaviors? It is helpful to think of cutting as an unhealthy coping tool to manage really big, painful feelings that otherwise cannot be verbally expressed. Cutting can provide a sense of calm for teens when they feel overwhelmed. It additionally offers a sense of control, especially if teens perceive external circumstances as chaotic. Oftentimes, cutting is a secretive behavior that happens behind closed doors. While parents should take a proactive approach to understanding the warning signs, it's important to note that cutting is not directly correlated with suicidal thoughts or the intention to commit suicide, nor is cutting a mental illness.

Cyberbullying has been linked with an increase in self-harming behaviors. The National Center for Education Statistics suggests that teenage girls are three times more likely to be cyberbullied than teenage boys. And according to the Journal of the American Academy of Child & Adolescent

Psychiatry, the trend toward self-harming is concerning, with more than 15 percent of teens engaging in this behavior. Research suggests that bullying is related to an increased risk of self-harming, yet while the risk exists, not all teens who are bullied engage in self-harming behaviors. If you observe or suspect that your teen has been cutting, please reach out for professional support.

THE STRUGGLE WITH BODY IMAGE

You've likely noticed the surge of increased awareness around healthy body image. We're seeing this with clothing campaigns that highlight body positivity by using a variety of models of different shapes and sizes, or with celebrities coming forward wearing no makeup or talking about their own struggles fitting into an unrealistic standard of beauty. While we've come a long way to being more inclusive and accepting, teen girls are absolutely still grappling with serious body-image issues.

Body image relates to having a positive or negative perception of any part of the body—this isn't strictly about weight and body shape. Most people struggle with body image or wish a specific part of their body was different. Yet, the concerns run deeper when statistics show that 65 percent of those under 18 years of age believe in an ideal body, and that one-fourth of one's self-esteem is tied to body image. What "ideal" means is subjective to the individual's desire, whether it's curvy, skinny, athletic, muscular, or something else.

Teens also struggle with not liking specific parts of their bodies. Dissatisfaction can lead to extreme dieting attempts, overexercising, and overfocusing on "flawed" areas of the body. These behavioral attempts by teens to feel satisfied with their body image can be exhausting and fuel the potential for negative decision-making. For example, teens may start looking for validation from others, which has the potential to lead teens to make poor choices to feel "good enough."

The pitfall here is that body image becomes linked with self-esteem, and unrealistic thoughts begin to govern how teens feel about themselves. It's common to hear teens talk unfavorably about their body image, with messages such as, "If I lost weight, I would be happy," critiquing parts of their body; "See this part here? I don't like it," they might say as they point, pull, or prod at the "offending" area. Body-image issues aren't exclusive to age, yet they do impact specific races and ethnicities differently. For example, researchers have found that Black teenagers are more likely than their white peers to purge due to dissatisfaction with their body image, and Latina females are more likely to experience bulimia compared to their non-Hispanic peers.

There's a tricky line between normalizing the fact that we all have parts about ourselves that we don't fully appreciate, while still providing a backdrop for a healthy body image. Teens constantly take in information about the ideal beauty standard, but most aren't questioning if the photos they see have been manipulated or what the average woman looks like in comparison to the model in front of them.

One step we can take is to encourage teens to question media messages around body image. For example, 96 percent of women and teens don't match models or actresses, because the average size for American women is 5 feet 4 inches and 166 pounds. You might also mention that 25 to 70 percent of one's body is determined by genetics. These kinds of discrepancies give teens an opportunity to challenge what they see in media with more factual information.

BEAUTY IS MORE THAN MEETS THE EYE

We've all heard the concept that beauty is more than just physical appearance, and that character is what makes someone beautiful. While this holds true, I also realize that this comes as an abstract concept for teens. Teens generally think in con-crete terms. Add social pressures to fit in, and teens become very aware of what is perceived as beautiful based on direct feedback from peers and indirect observations of various media influences.

As a society, we focus a lot on standards of beauty, and therefore allow others to place value on what it means to be beautiful. These standards are outside of ourselves, which means we're looking to external validation to make us feel good. This leads to an "I will feel better when . . . " mentality, suggesting that happiness will only come when this standard has been met and validated by others. Furthermore, this search for external validation exemplifies how we disconnect from our inner beauty and operate from a place of not recognizing or appreciating the beauty that lies within or those things that makes us unique. When we take time to emphasize inner beauty over physical beauty or even move in a direction of holding both as equal, we're changing a pattern, allowing personality and character to guide new standards of beauty.

When teens chase unrealistic ideas of what beauty is, focus-ing on physical appearance, they set themselves up to be extremely dissatisfied with who they are. On one hand, compar-ison can provide valuable information for our own benchmarks. However, when comparisons are unrealistic or unhelpful, we enter a dangerous territory that leads to painful feelings, including low self-worth, a devaluation of self, insecurities, and jealousy, that often breed resentment.

I've also observed that teens utilize physical beauty as an all-capturing indicator that someone's reality is perfect or without struggle. It's as though being beautiful has become synonymous with an easy life. As adults, we know this isn't true—teens, on the other hand, think in the here-and-now, thanks to their still-developing brain.

Some teens are vocal about beauty standards being a challenge for them, while others are more private. As a parent, it's important to acknowledge that a quiet demeanor doesn't necessarily mean that your teen isn't struggling with a poor body image. It could mean that they're internalizing their feelings; therefore, it's always a great idea to open this topic for discussion with your teen.

TAKING A DEEPER LOOK:
ARE EATING DISORDERS ON THE RISE BECAUSE OF SOCIAL MEDIA BEAUTY STANDARDS?

My daughter is obsessed with social media and loves to keep up with the latest beauty trends. Like most teens, she posts on social media and uses different filters. When she's off social media, I find her picking apart her "flaws," especially her body, and she goes through periods where she really watches what she eats and exercises more than usual. If you saw her, you'd think she was crazy. She's fit and has an athletic build, yet no matter what I say, she's not convinced that she looks great. I want her to feel healthy and not rely on extreme practices to feel good. Are eating disorders on the rise because of social media beauty standards?

Eating disorders are characterized by severe and persistent eating behaviors that are accompanied by over-whelming thoughts and emotions. There are six common types of eating disorders, which include anorexia nervosa, binge-eating disorder, bulimia nervosa, avoidant/restrictive food intake disorder, rumination disorder, and pica. Adolescent females and males are both impacted, but females are more than twice as likely to develop an eating disorder.

Eating disorders can cause serious health concerns, including, at their most extreme, death, and require specialized treatment programs.

While social media does not directly cause an eating disorder, there is a link between social media use and the development of a negative body image. Having a negative body image can lead teens to engage in dieting practices, excessive monitoring of their body, extreme exercise practices, and self-objectification, in which the teen sees themselves as an object to be evaluated based on their external attributes. One study found that self-objectification increases anxiety around one's own appearance, promotes thinness and overall shame, and hinders a positive mood. Additionally, individuals *recovering* from an eating disorder are more likely to be vulnerable to social media pressures.

Social media is a major influence on how teens perceive their bodies, providing countless opportunities for teens to compare themselves to others. This creates a disconnect from realistic expectations of what a healthy body is. And with puberty, teens are that much more aware of their bodies, especially in comparison to those of others, further perpetuating a negative body image. While there has been movement toward acceptance of all bodies, regardless of size, many teens continue to view themselves as overweight or heavy, as they still compare themselves to a thin body type.

STUDY PREP: YOUR POSITIVE PARENTING TIPS

- **ENCOURAGE YOUR TEEN TO COME TO YOU IF THEY ARE BEING BULLIED.** Being proactive and preventative is at the root of dealing with bullies. As a parent, you can be a tremendous support by listening to your teen and, if necessary, involving school or community leaders or the police. Talk to your teen about the following strategies if bullying occurs:
  - Look the kid bullying you in the eye and tell them to stop, calmly and clearly.
  - If you don't feel safe speaking up, walk away. Don't fight back. Instead, locate an adult to stop the bullying.
  - Speak to a trusted adult. It is healthier to share your feelings, and they can help you plan ways to stop the bullying.
  - Avoid places where bullying happens, and stick around adults and other kids.

- **CREATE ACCOUNTABILITY IF YOUR TEEN IS BULLYING.** A teen who bullies may know that their behaviors are hurtful; however, they may not connect that their actions are considered bullying. In addition to providing education on what bullying is, the harmful effects, why teens bully, and the different forms of bullying, explore what actions you can take to support your teen to change their behaviors. Invite your teen into this conversation by asking questions:
  - How do they feel when they are bullying?
  - Are they aware that their actions are considered bullying?

- If their friends bully, too, are there ways to disengage in these moments, or words they can say to prevent the bullying?

Bringing information into awareness of how they behave creates accountability to change future behaviors.

- **MAKE A PLAN TO DISENGAGE FROM CYBERBULLIES.** If your child is being cyberbullied, create an action plan with them. First, remind your teen to disengage from their bully online. Ignoring is a step in the right direction for your teen to take their power back. Support your teen in diminishing their exposure to the bullying, including blocking the accounts associated with the bully, changing personal account information, and ensuring that privacy settings are in place. It's also good practice to keep a record of any bullying activity. Be sure to praise your teen when they take these courageous steps.

- **ENGAGE AND VALIDATE.** If you suspect or observe that your teen has been cutting, a direct, non-reactive approach is best, such as, "I've noticed a few cuts on your arm. Have you been cutting yourself?" When your teen acknowledges the cutting, validate their pain, saying something like, "I can only imagine that you're having a lot of big feelings if you've felt the need to cut." Next, take steps to get your teen help. This should include consulting with a professional regarding how to best support your teen.

- **QUESTION IMAGES TOGETHER.** Teens are bombarded with various sources that suggest an ideal standard of beauty, and they draw conclusions from these sources. Engage your teen in an exercise: Together, look at different media sources, such as photos of models or general marketing, and ask them questions like, "What do you think this photo is trying to tell you about beauty standards?",

"When you see this picture, how do you feel?", and "Have you seen people in real life that look similar to this?" Show different weights, body shapes, races, ethnicities, facial features, etc.

- **RETHINK ADMIRABLE QUALITIES.** Teens draw an understanding of what beautiful is from surface-level, physical characteristics—we want to help change this pattern. Have your teen make a list of 5 to 7 people they know and think fondly of. Invite them to think about why they like these individuals or what they enjoy about them most. Encourage your teen to draw on areas that highlight personality traits and characteristics and list 5 admirable characteristics for each person. Once they're finished, engage your teen in a discussion about how beauty is more than what meets the eye, and use the evidence they shared to reinforce this message.

KEY TAKEAWAYS

Bullying and body-image concerns are an unfortunate theme for adolescents. The good news is that parents have the opportunity to support their teens in navigating these painful issues. Education is an important starting point for parents and teens alike to change how we approach these issues. Here are the key takeaways from this chapter:

- Bullying can happen in person, or behind closed doors via cyberbullying. Bullying impacts its victims differently, yet commonalities can include a change in mental health, social withdrawal, low self-worth, and mistrust of others. Online bullying is unique in that bullies can remain anonymous, humiliating content reaches a broader audience, and the internet never sleeps. It's important for parents to observe warning signs both for those being victimized (page 64) and for individuals perpetrating the bullying (page 65).

- Cutting is an unhealthy way of coping and a means to manage really big feelings that cannot be verbalized. Often rooted in a need for control, cutting can happen as a one-time incident or an ongoing, repetitive behavior. Cutting is not a mental health disorder and is not necessarily intended as a suicide attempt or correlated with suicidal thoughts. Teens being cyberbullied are more at risk for engaging in cutting behaviors; however, not all teens who are cyberbullied will resort to cutting.

- A negative body image involves a dissatisfaction with one's weight and/or body shape, and/or a dislike for any physical feature of the body. Teens continue to grapple with body image, even though the social climate has changed to endorse body positivity and openly address unrealistic beauty standards. Teens can benefit from exposure to new standards of beauty that support inner versus physical beauty, especially since teens tend to engage in comparison behaviors due to outside influences like social media. While parents fear that social media directly causes eating disorders, this is not the case, yet social media can negatively impact a teen's body image.

CHAPTER 6

TEACHING SEX ED TO TEENAGE GIRLS

I should caution that this chapter could cause discomfort, as the conversation about sex isn't always a comfortable one, nor one that should be treated lightly. Please give yourself permission to take this chapter at your own pace. My hope is that this information will provide a foundation for how to address educational information with your teen. While this chapter covers a lot, it's by no means exhaustive.

Parents often have many questions about how to address the topic of sex with their teens. We'll discuss:

- The various reasons that it's important to talk to your adolescent about sex

- How to have healthy conversations that address boundaries and how to best tailor these discussions to your teen

- Enthusiastic consent, which is different from consent, including how to help your daughter identify her boundaries and express these boundaries both verbally and assertively

- How classroom sex ed falls short, and some of the gaps that exist in how sex curriculum is taught

- The importance of talking to your teen about non-heterosexual sex, addressing sexual orientation and an inclusive approach to sexual health education

- Whether talking to your teen about sex will make them think it's okay to have it right away, and whether schools can enforce abstinence-only sex-ed classes

As always, our chapter will end with helpful parenting tips that can serve as a template to discuss sex with your teen.

WHY YOU SHOULD TALK TO YOUR TEEN ABOUT SEX (EVEN IF YOU DON'T WANT THEM TO HAVE IT)

Of all the topics I encourage parents to talk about, sex is one that creates many uncomfortable feelings. I also find that most parents don't know where to start when talking about sex, including what should be shared and how much education should be dispensed.

Realistically, conversations around sex will vary based on both the chronological and developmental age of your child, but since we know that some teens experiment sexually as early as junior high, it's clear that conversations about sex need to be a priority between teens and caregivers. Please note, your family's values and expectations will influence how you choose to proceed with your teen and what you share.

Through experience in my work with teens, I see that most teens are curious about sexual experiences, not so much because they want to have sex, but because questions about sex are a natural part of growing up. Caregivers are in a unique position to properly educate their teen on the various components of sex. Teens are closely observing their caregivers, picking up on their behaviors, yet actions don't always translate into concrete expectations. For example, teens can pick up on what a healthy relationship is by observing their caregivers; this doesn't mean that they can put into words what a healthy relationship is.

When we combine healthy actions with words, such as through expressing expectations, teens are more apt to integrate the information and use it later. For example, observing healthy interactions and engaging in discussions about expectations of when it's appropriate to have sex will serve as a foundation that teens can revisit when they're out of the home. Teens may not share the same beliefs that you have; however, the conversations they have with you will allow them to pause and reflect when challenging situations about sex arise.

Sex is confusing for teens, and they won't always feel comfortable having these conversations with peers. If they do, there's a risk for misinformation, as they're integrating information from the perspective of another developing teen. When caregivers take the lead, the educational aspects tend to be accurate, the parent has control over what is shared, and it normalizes for teens how confusing and multilayered sex is. It also allows teens to ask questions without the pressure of having to know everything.

With peers, teens are plagued with the potential question of "You don't know what (fill in the blank) is?" This can create further confusion and a comparison effect, which cues peer pressure. For instance, teens who feel as though they're behind in some way for not knowing may create their own inaccurate understanding of what something is, or will search for answers through the internet. Taking the lead role in talking with your teen also gives you direct access to the excitements and concerns that are arising for your teen around sex, which helps tailor conversations in a way that are most beneficial for your teen.

ENTHUSIASTIC CONSENT IS KEY

Consent is an individual's ability to say "yes" to something or to confirm that their permission has been granted. It has also been explained as "No means no," yet true consent has been re-termed as enthusiastic consent. For example, consent has largely involved a "Yes means yes" understanding of agreement, which has been faulted for perpetuating rape culture. Saying yes when feeling pressured into something is not consent. And consent doesn't account for situations in which someone is physically unable to express a no.

Enthusiastic consent moves beyond a simple "yes" or "no" and empowers each individual engaging in sexual activity to express that they're in fact enthusiastic about the sexual interaction. This model of consent reduces agreement ignited by peer pressure, allowing for open communication among all parties involved. Enthusiastic consent is about figuring out your own boundaries in relationships and learning ways to express those parameters. Discussions can start with asking your daughter, "What are things that you are willing and unwilling to do with a partner?" This isn't just about sexual acts and sex. We want teens to think about their boundaries when it comes to holding hands, kissing, and touching. You'll want to get specific, as these boundaries shift with time, mood, location, and partner.

The decision to have sex shouldn't be treated lightly, and teens need to feel comfortable turning down sex and being vocal about their needs. After your teen has addressed their own boundaries surrounding what feels right for them, the next step is to support your teen in vocalizing these boundaries. This piece takes practice, and the clearer your teen is on their boundaries, the easier it will be for them to step into their power. What words would they use to express their boundaries? How would they express their body language as they voice these boundaries? How does your teen feel when they talk about what they want and don't want?

Being nice is a standard consistent with female gender norms; consequently, passivity has been valued over truthfulness. This standard, along with enthusiastic consent as a necessary component, is shifting, giving girls "permission" to say what they really feel—this is why I strongly encourage parents to continue the conversations about boundaries, and practice expressing these boundaries.

TAKING A DEEPER LOOK: WILL TALKING TO YOUR TEEN ABOUT SEX MAKE THEM THINK IT'S OKAY TO HAVE IT RIGHT AWAY?

My daughter, who is fifteen, has started dating with our permission. I believe that she makes good decisions, yet I wonder about the pressures she could face when it comes to making decisions about engaging in sexual activities. I don't know if it's realistic to believe that she'll wait until she's married to have sex; however, I also don't think she's old enough now, or even in the next few years, to make such a big decision. I want to address the topic of sex with her, but I'm worried that this will lead her to think that I'm giving her permission to have sex. Will talking to your teen about sex make them think it's okay to have it right away?

Contrary to popular belief, talking to your teen about sex doesn't correlate to teens having sex right away. In fact, the opposite is true. Research suggests that talking to one's teen about sex is linked to teens waiting longer to have sexual intercourse. Additionally, when they do choose to have sex, they're more likely to use proper forms of birth control if they've had this talk with caregivers.

Talking with your teen about sex should cover more than what sex is and the different methods for birth control. Sex discussions should also address the concepts of consent versus enthusiastic consent, what sexual assault is, and the various ways they can create boundaries around their body.

There are many positives to discussing sex with your teen. First, teens get accurate information. Information from peers, media, and movies can be misguided or completely inaccurate, or address sex in comedic or harmful

continued >>

ways. For example, it's important that your teen has accurate information regarding why people choose to have sex or the potential consequences of having unprotected sex, including pregnancy or sexually transmitted diseases. And the more your teen observes that you are comfortable about topics of sex, the more likely it is that they will come to you with questions or if they're struggling with pressures to have sex. It's probable that your teen will be uncomfortable with this topic as well; having these conversations helps teens build a sense of assertiveness around sex. Assertiveness allows teens to understand their own expectations around sex and have the confidence to say no when faced with the choice to have sex when they're not ready.

WHERE TRADITIONAL SEX ED FALLS SHORT

"Proper" suggests something that is appropriate and effective, and "education" denotes a body of knowledge. Proper education implies that adequate information is provided, so individuals are given an opportunity to make informed choices with the information given. True education guides healthy decision-making. When it comes to traditional sex ed, one of the major shortcomings is that the education provided doesn't represent what happens in the real world, as the information is filtered through legislative laws specific to a region. This impacts teens in a few ways.

First, in the United States, teens don't receive the same curriculum across all states, and tremendous gaps exist for teens based on where they live. Because laws dictate what is taught, teens could be receiving information that is not medically accurate, that promotes abstinence, that is not LGBTQ+-inclusive, or that doesn't include education on consent.

If teens receive only partial information, the bigger question becomes, how are they supposed to understand their own sexuality or make effective decisions in real-life situations? Without a well-rounded educational framework, teens can only make decisions based on the information they have. For example, if a teen is taught that waiting until marriage to have sex is morally right and isn't given information on contraceptives, what outcomes could result if this teen still chooses to have sex? Granted, education doesn't guarantee that your teen will always make the best decision. But if they have well-rounded, factual information about sex, sexual health, prevention and birth control, sexuality, LGBTQ+-inclusive material, and consent, they have a better opportunity to make a sound decision simply because they know more.

Another critique of in-school sex education is that it's not an ongoing process. Sex education is typically provided as a one-time class between elementary school and high school, yet a lot changes for teens as they move through adolescence. The experience of a seventh grader is vastly different from that of a freshman in high school, and these two age groups will generally experience or question sexual health differently than a high school senior. Sex education needs to consider developmental transitions and integrate differently into each phase of adolescence. If sex education was designed to evolve with each phase of adolescence, teens would have continued opportunities to address relevant concerns or ask questions in real time.

Regardless of your geographic location, relying solely on the educational system to teach your teen about sex will inevitably result in gaps. To bridge these gaps, it's recommended that parents take an active approach in talking about sex with their teens. Start with where you and your teen feel most comfortable, in addition to what makes sense for your family's values.

IT'S IMPORTANT TO TALK ABOUT NON-HETEROSEXUAL SEX (EVEN IF YOU THINK YOUR TEEN IS STRAIGHT)

"Non-heterosexual" is an umbrella term for sexual orientation that is not heterosexual. Non-heterosexual includes gay, lesbian, bisexual, asexual, and any other identification that is not straight male or female. "Sexual orientation" denotes who an individual is attracted to emotionally, romantically, and sexually, and who they want to have a relationship with.

In addition to the identities listed previously, other possible identities or orientations include pansexual (attraction is not limited to one gender), queer (belonging to any sexual minority), and questioning or curious. I want to note that some teens like the idea of labels, while others don't, and some feel that these identities don't describe them at all. For these reasons and more, it is extremely important to respect each individual's preference.

In a recent global study, it was found that 1 in 5 young adults don't identify as heterosexual, highlighting even more of a necessity for sex education that is inclusive and accepting. As you'll read more about under "Taking a Deeper Look," fewer than 20 percent of states in the United States require that sex education address LGBTQ+-inclusive material, which means that our LGBTQ+ teens aren't receiving adequate or inclusive information on sex. Inclusive programs would support both LGBTQ+ teens and teens identifying as straight in receiving medically accurate information and understanding sexual orientation and gender identity. Ideally, these programs would address romantic relationships positively and address common myths and stereotypes associated with behavior and identity.

In my therapy work with parents, I often hear, "But my teen is straight." Truth is, in my work with teens, I have found that there are times when teens identify as straight to their loved ones, yet they truly identify with a different sexual orientation. Sharing one's sexual orientation makes someone extremely vulnerable, especially if teens fear negative reactions from their family and peers, or if they're just not ready to disclose. Research has shown that LGBTQ+ youth report having few trusted adults they can address their questions with. As a result, these youth turn to the internet for information that may not be age-appropriate or medically accurate. By addressing non-heterosexual sex, we provide teens who are still questioning, not ready to share, or curious, with a supportive foundation of acceptance, as well as factual information on sex, birth control methods, and overall sexual health.

TAKING A DEEPER LOOK: CAN SCHOOLS ENFORCE ABSTINENCE-ONLY SEX-ED CLASSES?

I've been hearing conversations among other parents about sex education and abstinence-only classes being offered in our schools. I didn't know this was something that I needed to think about, and I'm not sure how I feel about it. I have so many questions about what abstinence-only looks like, the curriculum they teach, and if this actually prevents kids from having sex. Can schools enforce abstinence-only sex-ed classes?

Sex education in the United States is not federally regulated; rather, policies and regulations are made at the state and local level. Each state forms its own rules about what school-based sex education looks like, including if abstinence is part of the curriculum, and how much abstinence is stressed.

Abstinence-only sex education programs teach students to not have sex until marriage and imply that sex outside of marriage can have harmful effects. This curriculum doesn't address birth control methods and has

continued >>

received scrutiny due to its lack of educational value in providing students with preventative information. Furthermore, when teens don't have the necessary information to make informed decisions about sex, their ability to make healthy decisions for themselves has been removed. This doesn't leave teens in a place of empowerment, and instead, relies on a curriculum that merely tells teens what they should and shouldn't do.

Laws dictating whether educational material is medically accurate and/or age-appropriate, and if birth control methods need to be included, vary by state. States can also decide if non-heterosexual sex is discussed; consequently, gaps exist for LGBTQ+ teens in states that don't cover this.

Planned Parenthood reports that:

- 15 states in the United States require that sex education be medically accurate.
- 26 states require that the information be age-appropriate.
- 37 states necessitate that abstinence is included in the curriculum.
- 9 states require that sex education addresses LGBTQ+-inclusive material.
- 7 states prohibit education on LGBTQ+ relationships.

The last statistic leaves those LGBTQ+-identifying teens at a higher risk for pregnancy, sexually transmitted diseases, and dating violence.

STUDY PREP: YOUR POSITIVE PARENTING TIPS

- **INVITE THE DISCOMFORT.** Talking about different aspects related to sex can be extremely awkward at first, yet I encourage you to "call it what it is" with your teen. Let your teen know you realize that these discussions are going to feel a bit weird sometimes, allowing both you and your teen to acknowledge your discomfort. Talk about *why* it feels awkward for you and your teen. Sharing your feelings of discomfort will provide a foundation for conversations moving forward, and the more conversations you have, the easier the topic of sex will be.

- **INVITE WRITTEN QUESTIONS.** Talking about and asking questions about sex can feel overwhelming. If this is the case, have no worries—there's a workaround. Sit down with your teen. Bring individual slips of paper you can fold after writing. Have your teen write down questions they have about sex, things they've heard, and worries they may have. I also invite parents to write down questions from the perspective of what you feel is important for your teen to know, such as "What are sexually transmitted diseases and how do you prevent them?" After you have written the questions together, fold them, and throw them in a container. Pick a paper from the container, read the question aloud, and answer it with age-appropriate and medically accurate information.

- **KEEP THAT CONTAINER.** Sexual topics are part of an ongoing conversation that will evolve as your teen matures. It can be helpful to have a space to address new concerns or questions that arise. Keep a container on hand that both you and your teen can add to, writing down new questions as they arise. This can remind your teen that sex is an ongoing topic, and that they will always have a place to come if they have any questions. Periodically, or once the container starts to fill, address what's been added. Over time, the container may not be needed, and your teen will know they can come directly to you with any questions or concerns.

- **PRACTICE BOUNDARY-SETTING.** Earlier in this chapter, it was recommended that your teen list their own boundaries when it comes to their interactions in relationships (page 82). Once they've written a list, help them practice vocalizing their needs within these boundaries. It can be helpful to provide a possible scenario and role-play what someone might ask or say in response to your teen. Pay attention to how your teen vocalizes their needs or wants. Are they talking with an assertive tone, or do they sound uncertain? What does their body language look like? Are they making eye contact or looking away or at the ground? It's important that teens learn to match their words with confident body language. Remind teens that this takes practice. The expectation is not necessarily to get it right on the first or second try, but to get comfortable over time, using their voice and body language to convey their boundaries.

- **FAMILIARIZE YOURSELF WITH THE CURRENT LANDSCAPE.** Since sex ed in the classroom falls short, I recommend educating yourself as a parent, particularly on LGBTQ+-inclusive sexual health. This includes gender identity, sexual orientation, health issues specific to LGBTQ+ youth, and challenges that LGBTQ+ teens are faced with when it comes to sexual education and sexual health. Even if your teen identifies as heterosexual, it's helpful to address these areas with your teen to further provide a landscape of inclusivity and acceptance.

KEY TAKEAWAYS

We've explored the various layers that encompass the topic of sex. Sex is not merely about sexual intercourse or heterosexual relationships. Sex education also includes a foundation in enthusiastic consent, understanding one's own boundaries for what they want in a relationship, providing accurate information that matches real life, and inclusivity. We touched on how talking to your teen about sex doesn't lead to teens having sex right away, and that inconsistencies exist in sex-ed curricula state by state as it relates to abstinence, medical accuracy, and inclusivity. As always, here are some key takeaways:

- Enthusiastic consent is not the same as consent. Enthusiastic consent is about ensuring that all partners are excited about engaging in different sexual activities, in which verbal expression is matched with body language. Sexual activities are not exclusive to sexual intercourse and include other aspects such as holding hands, kissing, and touching. It's recommended that teens identify their boundaries for relationships and practice vocalizing these boundaries.

- School-based sex ed has many shortcomings, in part due to the regulations that govern how sexual education is taught state by state, but also due to the fact that it's a one-time class rather than an ongoing curriculum that transitions with teens as they get older. Shortcomings include a lack of age-inappropriate information, medically inaccurate material, curriculum that is not LGBTQ+-inclusive, and gaps in information that leave teens open to making impactful real-life decisions without appropriate and well-rounded information.

- It's important for parents to discuss sex and sexual health with their teens, not only because schools fall short in providing adequate information, but also because teens have curiosities and questions that can't always be answered appropriately by peers or other outside sources. Parents can provide factual information in a shame-free environment, and convey that topics related to sex are a normal part of adolescent development.

CHAPTER 7

THE SELF-EXPRESSION OF TEENAGE GIRLS

The idea that we can show up exactly as we are and how we feel is empowering, and it makes us feel good. Teens are at a crucial developmental point when they're experimenting with their expression in a variety of ways. As a parent, you're going to have some moments where you think, "Oh goodness, this is different," yet for you to witness and support their changing expressions is a gift your teen will undoubtedly remember.

We'll start with understanding identity formation from the foundation of "trying on" different styles. "Changing looks" is bigger than just peer pressure—it requires a thorough understanding of how teens explore their identities and challenge gender roles, including how they express who they are to the outside world. We'll cover topics around:

- Gender expression, why teens challenge the status quo, and why they can be angsty

- How identity formation is a large part of adolescent development

- What is "normal," as opposed to significant changes and stressors that speak to a larger mental health issue

And don't forget to look for the helpful parenting tips at the end of this chapter.

UNDERSTANDING THE (MANY) POTENTIAL COSTUME CHANGES

Identity formation is critical during the adolescent years. Teens are developing a sense of who they are individually; they're also testing their values, beliefs, personality, ethics, sexual orientation, and gender identity against a larger social construct. Teens use their home environment, school setting, and other social arenas to navigate this process, often learning their own dos and don'ts, and what they stand for or don't, from these interactions.

"Trying on" and exploring different looks is common. It's a teen's way of experimenting with different parts of who they are, whether it's in small ways, such as changing their hairstyle, or through taking on a full makeover if they identify closely with a larger community such as punk or goth. For teens who are still developing confidence, testing a different look within the structure of a peer group is much more socially acceptable and comfortable than standing alone in one's appearance. In this way, peer pressure can play a positive role in supporting inclusion and healthy identity shifts.

Teens are meant to socialize, and peer pressure can swing as teens move between different groups. For example, teens know what's cool or acceptable to their peers, and engaging with different groups to increase social status is not uncommon, nor is trying on behavior or language that appears cool or mature in front of their peers. This may come with consequences if teens choose to engage in riskier behaviors, yet exploring decision-making and navigating pressures are part of the learning process that guides identity formation. In any situation, we all have choices, and understanding the way we make choices, what we do under certain pressures, and how we voice our concerns or don't, all make up who we are.

Changing interests or activities can help teens fine-tune what they like and dislike, and allows for teens to expand their horizons. Each teen is unique and has their own strengths and weaknesses. A teen may pursue an interest that highlights their strengths, or even fuels what could be perceived as a negative trait into something acceptable. Examples could include a teen who loves animals and signs up to volunteer at a local shelter, or an argumentative teen who joins the debate team. Different activities also allow teens to recognize where they aren't so strong, and give opportunities for teens to improve in these areas. While we want our teens to find pursuits they enjoy, learning that they don't like something is also valuable information. Teens can also engage in an activity that they otherwise wouldn't have tried, potentially sparking a new passion.

New experiences are consistently shaping how a teen understands the world around them—this means that teens need to, and will, constantly change. In this context, it becomes clear why teens benefit from engaging with different ideas, systems, communities, world views, etc.

EXPERIMENTING WITH GENDER EXPRESSION

Gender expression, also known as gender presentation, is how an individual chooses to outwardly express their gender to the world. This is different from sexual orientation and doesn't necessarily define one's gender. The expression of gender could be described as feminine, masculine, androgynous, or gender-neutral. Androgynous refers to an individual blending what is traditionally masculine and feminine, while gender-neutral isn't tied to masculinity or femininity. This section covers a brief overview of gender expression terms, but it's advised that loved ones continue their education to further expand their inclusive understanding.

Gender expression is not necessarily fixed. It falls on a spectrum and depends on how an individual is feeling; therefore, a teen can move between different expressions such as masculine one day, then gender-neutral the following day. Teens whose gender expression isn't fixed may choose to refer to themselves as gender-fluid.

Gender expression can include a person's clothes, hairstyle, mannerisms, voice, behaviors, and preferred pronouns. Parents can expect teens to identify with different pronouns including he/him, she/her, or they/them, or being called by their birth name or a chosen name. Using desired pronouns and an individual's chosen name shows your teen that you accept them as they are and provides a space for inclusivity.

It's important to acknowledge that gender expression can challenge gender roles. Gender roles are assigned expectations for how a person is "supposed" to behave or dress, based on their assigned or perceived sex. For example, a male could be considered to be challenging these roles if they choose to wear a dress: a behavior that has largely been an acceptable behavior for females only. While gender expression has been tied to social activism and challenging social norms, many teens are simply exploring their gender expression.

Gender expression plays an important role in one's identity and overall sense of wellness. If teens feel supported in their expressions, they're more likely to experience positive mental health. Parents often question how to best approach gender expression. The good news is, caregivers can be supportive without feeling the exact same way as their teen. Teens want to feel comfortable, and creating a strong sense of self requires looking at different ways to be oneself. Teens may find they're more comfortable only expressing certain aspects of who they are until they feel confident sharing more; they may also still be figuring out the rest of who they are.

TAKING A DEEPER LOOK:
MY DAUGHTER REFUSES TO WEAR MAKEUP AND PREFERS TO WEAR TOMBOYISH CLOTHES TO SCHOOL. DOES THAT MEAN SHE'S GAY?

My daughter, age fourteen, isn't a typical girly girl. She seems to just throw on whatever is easy to wear and goes to school. Since I can remember, she has preferred to play sports and get dirty, and it's been a struggle introducing more feminine activities to help her fit in more. She does have a lot of friends, although they're mostly boys. I have always referred to her as a tomboy and wonder if my efforts to make her more girly are counterproductive. I'm not sure what to do. She refuses to wear makeup and prefers to wear tomboyish clothes to school. Does that mean she's gay?

Someone's preference for certain clothing or makeup (or lack thereof) doesn't correlate with their sexual orientation. There's no behavioral or appearance checklist to determine if your teen identifies as gay or any other sexual orientation. The only way you'll know if your teen identifies as gay is if they share their sexual orientation with you. A teen's "coming out" is a very personal and vulnerable choice that needs to happen on their own timeline, and I don't recommend directly asking your teen if they're gay.

The deeper context of this question embodies gender norms and stereotypes. Gender norms are ideas of how females and males need to behave based on their biological or perceived sex, whereas gender stereotypes are general traits and attributes that males and females are perceived to exclusively possess. Essentially, these two

continued >>

terms are submerged in judgments about what we expect of individuals who are assigned male or female at birth, and our perceived notions of what it means to be feminine and masculine. These judgments of how each gender is expected to show up in the world can clash with gender identity, which is the gender someone chooses. Gender identity can be different from one's gender assigned at birth; this goes back to one's personal choice.

It's also important to remember, when we make judgments of what it means to be masculine and feminine, we're inherently telling our teens that they need to conform to ideas and behaviors that could go against what they want or what feels comfortable to them. As parents, we want the opposite—we want our teens to express their uniqueness confidently.

IS IT A MENTAL HEALTH ISSUE?

Sometimes it's hard for parents to tell what's what, especially when we have to decode and integrate different pieces of information, like what's considered "normal" adolescent development; where does "normal" development end and a need for concern enter the picture; or if there's something more, such as anxiety, depression, or another mental health concern. These are all great questions, and one key factor to look for is a significant change or changes in mood, behavior, or performance.

The term "significant" is subjective; this isn't about comparing your teen to another teen, but rather comparing your teen's previous mood, behaviors, and performance to their current state in these three areas. "Significant" is also relative; it can signify drastic changes, but also smaller changes that cue your parent radar that something doesn't feel quite right. Drastic changes will be easier to observe, such as academic concerns due to increased fighting or a sudden refusal to go to school, substance use, expressing thoughts of suicide or a suicide attempt, panic attacks, or crying episodes that seem to come out of nowhere. Some more subtle changes can include changes in personality, sleep patterns, or eating behaviors; withdrawal or isolation from family and/or friends; difficulty concentrating and paying attention; fatigue and loss of energy; physical symptoms such as stomachaches or headaches; and sadness or feelings of being overwhelmed.

As you read this, you might feel as though your teen could meet some of these criteria. It's important to take into context what is happening in their inner world and their outer landscape. Stressors play a role here. For example, it's quite normal for a teen to experience poor sleep the evening before an exam, yet it's concerning if they experience panic attacks and nausea the entire week leading up to an exam. Other stressors to keep in mind include life changes, such as moving to a new home or divorce; environmental shifts such as large crowds or entering a quiet space; sudden changes including a pop quiz or the unexpected loss of a pet; social factors such as maintaining friendships or experiencing bullying; and traumatic events such as being in a car accident or witnessing a scary event.

Much of this decoding is about knowing your teen and keeping an open dialogue with them as well as their teachers and other communities that interact with your teen. This way, if something feels off or different, you can confidently reach out to ask for their observations of your teen's mood, performance, and behaviors, and any changes they may have observed. Oftentimes, these other communities have insights that we can't know because we aren't in that environment. If you're unsure what to do next or aren't clear on what's "normal" development, it's best to reach out to a trained professional.

WHY THE ANGSTY AESTHETIC
IS SO APPEALING

I often hear these questions from caregivers: "Why does my teen question everything?" and "Why are they being so difficult?" These questions carry themes of a rebellious teen who challenges the status quo and societal norms, and I assure you, it is all very purposeful from a developmental standpoint. Adolescence is a time of asserting independence, creating a separate identity, and testing authority figures and boundaries.

These different ways of asserting oneself, while frustrating for loved ones, are all forms of learning. As teens grow in an age where activism is palpable, they have numerous opportunities to question the current standards of what's happening in the world. Through these avenues, teens get to identify what they stand for and create a narrative for who they are or want to be. Activism and questioning the status quo provide an environment of acceptability for teens to rebel, because many of these outlets welcome confrontation. Standing up for a movement can create a healthy space for teens to find their voice and engage in a collective mission. We know that teens want to belong and be included, and joining a group allows teens to feel connected, while developmentally learning the fundamentals of problem-solving, resiliency, and working within a group dynamic.

As teens navigate the balance of becoming their own individual person and wanting social acceptance, angst becomes part of a greater outlet for creative expression. Art forms provide this freedom of expression, whether it's through painting, music, performance, writing, joining a movement, or yes, self-expression. Think about this for a few minutes. Teens are boxed into toeing a line, following rules, and knowing that if they test a boundary or cross a limit, consequences await. For the most part, they are governed by rules throughout their day within the academic setting, societal standards, and household boundaries. To show angst or rebellion in the ways they present and express themselves allows a much-needed sense of freedom.

We know that rules are good and necessary, yet when a teen is working hard to develop into their own person, creativity becomes a welcome opportunity to dismiss the rules and test the boundaries. Creativity is limitless and allows for teens to be emotionally expressive. Emotions are the dominant force as the brain continues to mature, and artful expressions don't ask emotions to be regulated. Art forms give teens permission to fuel their emotions into creativity. Teens can express anger, sadness, and other discomforting emotions in ways that don't necessarily require words.

TAKING A DEEPER LOOK:
MY DAUGHTER WEARS A LOT OF BLACK AND LISTENS TO MUSIC ABOUT DEATH. IS SHE DEPRESSED?

My daughter, who's a freshman in high school, recently started wearing dark colors and almost gothic-like clothing, and listens to dark music that feels really heavy and sad. As her parent, I don't love the look and would prefer that she wear brighter colors, but she pushes against the majority of my suggestions. She's a great kid overall and has friends, yet I don't know what to think of her darker appearance and depressing choice in music. Is she depressed?

Your daughter's preference for dark clothing and choice of music, both together or alone, are not signs of depression. From a clinical standpoint, a diagnosis of depression entails having at least 5 of the following criteria (the first criterion is mandatory) for two weeks or more:

continued >>

- A depressed mood most days or a loss of interest or pleasure in most activities
- A significant change in weight including weight gain or weight loss without dieting efforts
- Fatigue or loss of energy
- Difficulty concentrating
- Recurrent thoughts of death or suicide
- Feelings of worthlessness
- Difficulty sleeping or oversleeping
- Either an increase in physical activity that has no purpose, such as pacing, or slowed movements or speech that is observable to others

Listening to music about death isn't necessarily something to worry about, particularly if it's an isolated behavior or if your teen has an otherwise healthy lifestyle. However, if your teen exhibits some or most of these symptoms, or engages in other risky behaviors such as substance use, along with listening to music that has themes of death or suicide, this warrants talking with a professional who can help assess the needs of your teen.

While the research is mixed regarding whether music increases a teen's risk of suicide, it's best to address death-themed music choices with teens as part of a preventative approach. Openly ask your teen, "What do you like about this music?" or "In what ways does this music feel relatable?" There could be a variety of reasons; you won't know unless you ask them directly.

STUDY PREP: YOUR POSITIVE PARENTING TIPS

- **ENCOURAGE SELF-EXPRESSION.** Expressing individuality, including gender, doesn't always come with a high level of confidence. Some teens find it easy to express themselves freely, but what can you do if your teen isn't comfortable? Support your teen to take small steps to express themselves. You can ask, "If you felt very confident in yourself, how would you express yourself? What would this look like?" Have your teen take note of what feels like an easy and comfortable first step, and what will bring them joy.

- **PUT A SPIN ON "NEGATIVE" TRAITS.** We love our teens, but we don't always love every characteristic, especially if these traits carry the potential for a negative response. A few examples are a teen who questions everything, is naturally stubborn, or likes to argue. As the caregiver, take the time to step back, observe the "negative" trait, and think about how this trait could be a positive thing. For example, a stubborn teen is likely to stay true to what makes sense for them personally and is more apt to set boundaries with others. These "negative" traits fall on a spectrum and sometimes need additional consideration to bring them back into balance. So, if your teen is tipping the scale in one direction, it might be helpful to point out to them how the trait is a positive thing, but that there may be times when this characteristic gets them into trouble or hurts others' feelings.

- **DIG DEEP AND CHALLENGE YOUR PERSPECTIVE.** When it comes to addressing topics around gender, sexuality, and orientation, it's common for loved ones to grapple with the different definitions, as well as why these labels are necessary. As a caregiver, give yourself permission to understand your own perspective on these topics. I find that most parents don't have all the educational resources and/or haven't taken an internal look at their own experience. Doing so will help you separate your own experience from that of your teen, and decreases the likelihood that your personal sentiments come out in ways that can be detrimental to your teen's experience.

- **HAVE A BASELINE FOR COMPARISON.** When observing significant changes in your teen around mood, behavior, and performance, it's helpful to have a baseline of comparison already in place. If you occasionally take inventory of where your teen stands emotionally, socially, academically, physically, mentally, spiritually, etc., you'll be better able to identify when significant changes occur that may require intervention. This inventory can be done through your own assessments, observations from others, and talking with your teen regularly about how things are going.

- **CHANGE THE NARRATIVE ON TESTING LIMITS.** Pushing boundaries isn't just about making others upset, although it's easy to do that. The next time your teen tests a boundary, get curious. Ask yourself, "What are the possible reasons that my teen is testing the boundary right now?" or "Are there any stressors or external factors to take into consideration here?" Sometimes you can engage directly with your teen by asking, "I can see you're testing this limit right now—can you help me understand where you're coming from?"

- **SUPPORT CREATIVE OUTLETS AND PASSIONS.** Find ways to encourage your teen to creatively express themselves, and/or find resources that will support your teen to strengthen a skill set or develop in an area that isn't so strong or that sparks their interest. Look in the community and online, then have a conversation with your teen about what looks interesting and encourage them to use creative spaces to further process their feelings, ideas, beliefs, etc.

KEY TAKEAWAYS

To fully embody who we are takes courage. Teens face internal pressures; fear judgment from peers, the larger community, and society; and are highly attuned to what is acceptable to their family of origin, so to share the entirety of who they are isn't the easiest task. Here are some key takeaways:

- Maintaining social status, gaining acceptance, appearing mature, fine-tuning likes and dislikes, and strengthening skills are part of a bigger picture that comprises a teen forming their identity. Peer pressure also plays a role as teens "try on" different styles that extend beyond wanting to belong. Feeling accepted and confident by testing a style within a group becomes a safe alternative, compared to being the only one standing out.

- Gender expression is how an individual chooses to express their gender to the outside world. To adolescents, exploring gender expression is part of identity formation and a means to showcase their true being. Gender expression is not fixed—it falls on a spectrum and is dictated by personal choice. Gender expression is different from sexual orientation and doesn't necessarily define one's gender.

- "Normal" is a subjective term—every individual has their own normal, and it's not good practice to compare a teen to other peers. "Significant" is a relative concept that helps guide potential next steps when comparing your teen's previous mood, behavior, and performance to their current presentation in these three areas. Stressors will also point to what level of additional support your teen may need.

- Teens aren't challenging the status quo for fun, although they sometimes take delight in testing limits. Pushing boundaries is part of how teens learn to assert independence and create their own separate identity. Different art forms also support this process, as creative expression becomes an outlet to showcase angst and feelings that otherwise are asked to be regulated.

CHAPTER 8

TALKING ABOUT DRUGS & ALCOHOL WITH TEENAGE GIRLS

Parents inevitably have lots of questions when it comes to talking with teens about alcohol and drugs. There are many considerations, including where to start, what to talk about, and what to share from your own past experimentation or use. This chapter covers many of these aspects; however, I do recommend that parents expand their understanding of the current alcohol and drug climate beyond this book, as trends are constantly changing.

THIS CHAPTER WILL COVER:

- The different reasons teens choose to drink
- How the teenage brain is affected by alcohol, in both the short term and long term
- Today's drug culture, including some of the drugs teens could encounter
- What situations and behaviors place teens at risk and warning signs to look out for
- Vaping and its uncertain long-term effects

- Whether parties with alcohol are okay if they're at home

- Whether a caregiver should divulge their past drug use

While there are many helpful parenting tips regarding how to talk about drugs and alcohol, I have provided those that I've found to be the most supportive and beneficial toward the end of this chapter.

TO DRINK OR NOT TO DRINK IS ALWAYS THE QUESTION

The choice to drink or not is one of the many pressures teens will encounter. According to the National Center for Drug Abuse Statistics, the most commonly used substance among teens is alcohol. Teens drink for different reasons. Drinking becomes appealing when social pressures interact with a developing brain and a lack of parental supervision, especially when teens enter larger gatherings or a party setting.

Peer pressure is one of the more apparent reasons leading teens to drink. Fitting in becomes a priority during adolescence. When a teen's peers are drinking, the appeal becomes magnified. Since the prefrontal cortex is still developing, teens won't necessarily think about the relationship between their actions and consequences. The desire to feel accepted will override rational thinking. Other top reasons include the availability of alcohol and curiosity. If teens see their friends drinking, they may drink simply because it's present or because they are misinformed about the real consequences. Some teens may understand the dangers of drinking, but want to find out for themselves what happens when they drink.

As adults, we know that alcohol lowers inhibitions, but teens aren't necessarily making this connection. Media's portrayal of alcohol as a means to "let loose" gives teens a misguided message that alcohol is okay to use. For teens who want a boost in confidence, alcohol appears to provide an avenue to increase socialization and have more fun. Johns Hopkins Research Center has shown that 93 percent of movies that teens watch show alcohol use being portrayed as "not a big deal." This statistic suggests that the way teens observe and consume media sources will influence their engagement with alcohol. Other media sources impacting alcohol use include advertisements and celebrity endorsements.

Drinking is also used as an unhealthy coping mechanism. Individually, teens have unique experiences that challenge their internal resources. Knowing that alcohol can provide instant gratification to feel better or obtain temporary relief is especially rewarding to the part of the brain associated with pleasure-seeking. For some, alcohol becomes an avenue to escape a hard reality. These realities could include conflict in the home, financial struggles, or a family member's illness. Alcohol, from this perspective, provides teens with short-term comfort, but the long-term consequences are not considered. Additionally, alcohol can be used to self-medicate due to a teen's experience with mental health or emotional concerns. Research has shown that those who struggle with mental illness are more vulnerable to drinking.

Adolescents face many pressures, and we've covered several of them throughout this book. One additional example to take into consideration is parental pressure. Some examples of parental pressure include academic expectations to excel, pressures to perform in extracurricular activities, and direct or indirect expressions around perfection and success. These pressures tie into a teen's choice to rebel through drinking. Teens have a keen sense for what makes their caregivers tick, so if the opportunity to drink is present, it's possible that teens will take on an "I don't care what happens" attitude.

THE EFFECTS OF ALCOHOL
ON THE TEENAGE BRAIN

As we learned in chapter 2, the teenage brain is still developing—so what impact will alcohol have? The simple answer is that the choices teens make around alcohol carry both short-term and long-term implications. For starters, think about the brain as separate parts that together make up the whole—each individual part needs to work effectively, and also work with the other parts of the brain.

The hippocampus is affected by the consumption of alcohol. The hippocampus is in charge of learning and memory, which in part is why people experience "blackouts" or have difficulties recalling memories after a night of drinking. The long-term impact can be serious. Research shows that the hippocampus in adolescents who drink liberally and often is smaller than that of their peers. Learning and memory are vital skills used well into adulthood, and early drinking behaviors can impact performance at school, work, and other environments.

The prefrontal cortex—the part of the brain responsible for impulse control and rational thinking—is also impacted by drinking. A lack of judgment, irrational decision-making, and engaging in risky behaviors are all issues related to the prefrontal cortex. Poor judgment can lead to drunk driving. Statistics show that 8.2 percent of high school students have driven drunk at least once, and, on average, 8 teens die every day in the United States due to drunk driving. Risky behaviors include, but are not limited to, engaging in sexual activities, unintentional accidents, and suicide. If this part of the brain becomes damaged over time, overall judgment could be affected into the adult years.

The hypothalamus manages how our physical body responds to stress, including our "fight or flight" response. This part is also still developing during adolescence, and when alcohol is introduced, the fight or flight response doesn't work as effectively, since the normal hormonal response that triggers it gets subdued.

Coordination, controlled by the cerebellum, is inhibited by alcohol as well, which accounts for poor balance and muscle coordination experienced by teens who drink. The medulla, which controls breathing and the heartbeat, also becomes impaired. One of the reasons this is more dangerous for teens is because teens tend to drink more in a shorter period of time, as compared to adults.

TAKING A DEEPER LOOK:
SOME PARENTS LET KIDS HAVE PARTIES WITH ALCOHOL AS LONG AS THEY'RE HOME. IS THIS OKAY?

As my teens get older, they're asking to go to more parties. While the household expectation is that the peer hosting needs their parents present, and we expect our teens to make responsible decisions, I also know that drinking may be widely accepted by their peers and even the parents. I want my kids to have fun, yet I worry about what happens at these parties if parents aren't really home, or if parents are home but are more permissive than I would like. Then I wonder if I should be the parent allowing parties at my house. Is it okay to allow teens to have alcohol at parties as long as a parent is present?

No, you should not provide alcohol to teens or minors. While laws vary in the United States, with each state governing underage drinking, the concerns extend beyond legal ramifications. First, you're responsible for what happens in your home; therefore, if you permit drinking and something bad happens, the accountability lies with

continued >>

you. The reality is that teens vary in how they choose to experiment with alcohol—some will engage full-force without truly knowing the consequences of their consumption, some will try one drink, and others will choose not to drink. With alcohol experimentation falling on a spectrum, as a parent you cannot account for how kids will react to alcohol or if they will behave responsibly, including choosing not to drink and drive or choosing to get in the car with a sober driver.

Second, you're making a choice to provide a substance that other teens and parents are likely not comfortable with. In my work, I hear of parents who prefer that their teen experiments under their roof versus a setting outside the home. If you share this sentiment, it doesn't mean that all other parents support this line of thinking.

It's also important to consider that you don't know an individual's experience around alcohol. You may be offering alcohol to a child for whom addiction runs in their family, to a teen that's taking medication, or to a teen in recovery. The reality is that you don't know everyone's circumstance, which means you're playing a dangerous game. If you're questioning serving alcohol, take a moment to think about why you considered this as an option. What comes up for you?

THE TRUTH (NOT D.A.R.E.) ABOUT DRUGS

Talking to teens about drugs is no easy feat, especially when this topic is so complex and the culture of what to look out for constantly changes. For these reasons, one of my recommendations is for caregivers to remain educated on the latest drug trends and facts, not just for drug prevention, but also to support their own credibility when addressing the realities of substance use with their teen.

Marijuana, prescription medication, and opioids continue to be areas of concern for different reasons. Marijuana has largely been considered a "gateway drug," implying that those who use it will begin to use other drugs. There is a correlation between marijuana use and other drug use, in that those who use marijuana are more likely to use other drugs. Prescription medications are highly addictive, which is why there are growing regulations around how medical doctors prescribe and monitor these drugs. Some highly addictive prescription drugs include Xanax, Oxy-Contin, Vicodin, Adderall, and codeine.

Opioids have been deemed a national public emergency in the United States. In 2019, studies showed that opioid-overdose-related deaths increased by 500 percent since 1999 among 15- to 24-year-olds. Opioids encompass some of the prescription drugs listed previously, in addition to heroin and fentanyl. Another category to address is that of stimulants, such as amphetamines and cocaine; however, studies show that teens are more likely to abuse prescription stimulants such as Adderall and Ritalin. While this information can be extremely scary, please keep in mind that experimenting during adolescence doesn't mean that a teen will become addicted or remain an addict into adulthood. It does, however, support the notion that parents need to be aware of the different drugs and how addictive each one can be.

As a loved one, what should you look out for and what are the risk factors? Warning signs include:

- Finding drugs or drug paraphernalia

- Smelling unusual or different odors on your teen

- Dilated pupils

- Rapid weight loss

- Changes in eating and sleeping patterns

- Changes in mood

- Behavioral problems

- Academic changes

- Lying behaviors

- Isolation or withdrawal

  Risk factors for substance use include:

- Lack of parental supervision

- Severe disciplinary actions by caregivers

- Lack of communication between parent and teen about what drugs are, their side effects, and the consequences of using drugs

- Permissiveness, such as caregivers giving their teens permission to engage in alcohol or drug use

- Family history of alcohol or drug use

  Prevention is key. In addition to staying up-to-date on drugs and drug culture, other measures include:

- Educating your teen on substance use

- Discussing household expectations and clear boundaries on what will happen if they engage in drug use

- Safe storage of any prescription medications so that teens don't have access

- Being aware of your teen's whereabouts and knowing their friends

- Monitoring for any changes in behavior or performance that cause concern

If you suspect that your teen is experimenting with drugs or using regularly, please consult with a professional immediately and get your teen the necessary help.

YES, YOU SHOULD BE CONCERNED ABOUT VAPING

Vaping is a common concern among caregivers—for good reason—but what exactly is it and how does it work? Vaping, similar to smoking cigarettes due to the action of inhaling and exhaling, is the inhaling of vapor that gets extracted from nicotine, flavorings, and other chemicals. The vapor is generated by an electronic cigarette, also known as an e-cigarette, or other device. E-cigarettes are battery-powered devices that contain cartridges or pods, and the cartridges are filled with liquid that contains the nicotine, flavoring, and other chemicals.

Other devices used for vaping include tanks and mods, or items that resemble cigars, pipes, pens, and USB memory sticks. The fact that these devices look like everyday items makes it easy for teens to hide their vaping from parents. While the long-term consequences of vaping are not yet clear, we do know that nicotine is directly linked to different health issues including death. Additionally, the vapor, which contains different chemicals, gets directly inhaled into the lungs, which is not expected to be healthy over time or with increased use.

Vaping has become popular among teens for different reasons. Vaping doesn't leave behind a strong smell in the same way tobacco cigarettes do, so it can be difficult for parents and school personnel to detect. Also, vaping has been marketed in a way that translates into two messages to teens: Vaping is harmless compared to tobacco cigarettes, and vaping is less addictive than regular cigarettes. These messages aren't true. Research suggests that e-cigarettes are linked to chronic lung disease and asthma, and vaping is just as addictive as smoking tobacco cigarettes. What's more, some findings share that teens who engage in vaping are more likely to try other nicotine products, such as regular cigarettes.

It's important for caregivers to know that other drugs that have been found to be inhaled through e-cigarettes include LSD (acid), ketamine (a drug that induces anesthesia), and GHB (a sedative) due to their abilities to vaporize. Marijuana can also be vaped using a concentrated form. This information isn't meant to scare you; it's to provide a broader understanding regarding the potential risks associated with vaping. It's helpful to ask your teen what they know about vaping. Because teens may be misinformed, it's encouraged to discuss what vaping is and the associated risks.

TAKING A DEEPER LOOK: SHOULD I BE HONEST WITH MY TEEN ABOUT MY PAST RECREATIONAL DRUG USE?

I'm not sure what the best approach is with my teen, who is fifteen. Realistically, I know that when she's out, she will be exposed to peers who are drinking or experimenting with other substances like marijuana, but where do I draw the line with sharing my own past use of experimenting with drugs? Do I wait until she asks me about it, or do I come clean and tell her up front? I don't want to lie, but I don't know that sharing is in her best interest or if my honesty will send a message that it's okay to try drugs. Should I be honest with my teen about my past recreational drug use?

There is no one-size-fits-all approach to sharing your own past recreational drug use with your teen—the answer is, it depends. It is recommended that caregivers educate their teens about alcohol and drugs, especially since we know that experimentation with alcohol and drugs is a normal part of adolescence. This is not to suggest that teens should not be held accountable for their choices. Education includes talking about peer pressure; the consequences of using substances, including how they impact behavior and decision-making capabilities; and family expectations around recreational drug use.

In order to make an informed decision on whether you should disclose your own past history, take these factors into consideration. First, did your teen ask? Generally, teens won't ask for information that they don't want to know. If your teen hasn't asked, you shouldn't feel pressured to share. Second, what is the intention behind your reason to share? As parents, we sometimes get caught up in sharing because we think we're supposed to, yet I encourage you to get clear on why you want to share. Is the reason for you or for your teen? Are there any potential consequences in sharing?

For example, if you have a naturally rebellious teen who has already experimented, could sharing your story lead them to feel more entitled to use because they know you have? Consider the personality of your teen. Will they be responsible with knowing your past use, and are they clear on why you've chosen to share (for example, addressing peer pressures)? Please know that you can still provide an effective education to your teen on substance use without disclosing your own history.

STUDY PREP: YOUR POSITIVE PARENTING TIPS

- **PLAN FOR PREVENTION.** Preventing drug use calls for an open-door policy and ongoing conversations, with attention to addressing peer pressures. Resisting peer pressure takes practice, and also knowing your audience and setting. Create scenarios with your teen where they practice declining and saying "no," and teach them how to know their peers. For example, certain friends will be more apt to engage in peer pressure or make extra efforts to convince your teen that using a substance is an okay choice. Ask your teen to think about which friends those are. Prevention doesn't have to be on the spot. Prevention is also saying no to an invitation to a gathering or walking away when instincts tug at your teen to say something is wrong.

- **OFFER AND DISCUSS LIFELINE OPTIONS.** When saying no becomes too overwhelming, have an escape plan in place with your teen. Let them know they can call or text you if something goes awry or if they encounter a sticky situation. If your teen makes a poor choice, like drinking, and follows it with a positive one, such as calling for a ride instead of driving home under the influence, make sure you praise the healthy choices being made. It's also good to create some "what-if" scenarios, providing your teen with problem-solving options. For instance, "If your driver drinks too much, what can you do?" or "If things get out of hand and you feel uncomfortable, what are your options?"

- **EXPLORE THE SUBJECT TOGETHER.** Take time to educate your teen on the short- and long-term consequences of alcohol and drug use. Don't assume they already know. There are a lot of great online resources, and some sites are specifically tailored for teens. Sit together and review these sites. The goal is not to instill fear, but to create a larger understanding and help cement the foundation of prevention.

- **PLANT SEEDS OF WISDOM THEY CAN CARRY.** As a parent, you can't control what your teen does when they're not with you. This knowledge can create a sense of fear, especially when you know the pressures teens can face around alcohol and drugs. While teens don't retain everything—and sometimes they actively ignore what we tell them—the continued messages and conversations you have with them have the potential to be mentally retrieved when they're out of the home. Think of every conversation as an opportunity to plant an idea. They're taking in more than we sometimes give them credit for.

- **DON'T WAIT TO ACT.** I cannot stress enough the importance of asking for support from a professional if you suspect that your teen is using alcohol or drugs. Please don't wait until the behaviors reach a destructive point. Trust your instincts and act. Substance abuse and addiction are serious issues that require specialized intervention. The earlier you seek help, the better for your teen. Please check out the resources section (page 130) for guidance.

- **CONSIDER HOW SHARING MAKES SENSE.** I want to circle back to the question "Should I be honest with my teen about my past recreational drug use?" (page 120). After you've addressed your motivation behind wanting to share and have concluded that sharing makes sense, or when your teen has a specific question about your past use from a neutral standpoint (meaning asking when they're not upset or angry), follow these guidelines:
  - Be honest and address the context in which you used, such as peer pressure or a rebellious moment.
  - Address the consequences of your actions.
  - Talk about how you observe your own choices now, from the perspective of an adult.

KEY TAKEAWAYS

The adolescent years pose countless opportunities and challenges for teens. Among those is the choice to experiment with
alcohol and drugs. Doing so presents the possibility of bigger
consequences, and for this reason, teens need to be educated
so that they have the option to make informed and positive
choices. While it's common for teens to face the pressures to
drink and experiment with substances, this "normal" part of
development still requires prevention practices and up-to-date
knowledge to guide ongoing discussions between caregivers
and teens. Here are the key takeaways from this chapter:

- Alcohol is the most-used substance by teens and has
  both short- and long-term consequences. The effects
  impact the developing brain, including the hippocampus,
  prefrontal cortex, hypothalamus, cerebellum, and medulla.
  Alcohol additionally impacts motor functioning, learning
  and memory, coordination, decision-making, the fight or
  flight response, breathing, and the potential for engaging in
  risky behaviors.

- Marijuana, prescription medications, opioids, and stimulants are drugs that present serious concerns for different
  reasons. Marijuana has been labeled the "gateway drug,"
  prescription drugs are highly addictive, and opioids are
  reported to be a national concern due to alarming rates of
  overdose. It's important for caregivers to remember that a
  teen's decision to experiment with drugs doesn't necessarily mean that they will become addicted, yet the potential
  for addiction can increase based on risk factors.

- Vaping doesn't carry a smell in the same way tobacco cigarettes do, and because vaping devices look like regular items, teens are easily able to hide their use from parents and other adults. Vaping is still misunderstood, yet it is addictive and has been linked to chronic lung disease and other illnesses. Other drugs can be inhaled through e-cigarettes, including LSD, ketamine, and GHB, while marijuana can be vaped in a concentrated form.

GRADUATION & BEYOND

Before we jump into summarizing the last eight chapters, I want you to take a few minutes for yourself. Pause for just a moment and take inventory.

- What stood out most for you?

- What topic is a priority for you or one that will most benefit your teen at this time?

- What topic area caused some discomfort or further questions?

- What section(s) made the most sense to you?

These questions are just a few stepping stones for recommendations on how to best address these topics as you move forward on your journey with your daughter. But first, let's summarize what we learned.

Many things are happening for your teen, and the developmental backdrop is massive. Teens experience physical, social, and cognitive changes, and they face many pressures. Peer pressure, possible experimentation with substances and sex, and performance expectations from school, home, and social media are just a few of the pressures. Add in a cultural landscape that is consistently changing, and teens are charged with the developmental task of discovering their own individual identity despite these formidable constructs.

We have to incorporate how girls communicate their feelings and learn how to set boundaries by identifying their own limits, wants, and needs, as well as how they can learn to be empowered to say "yes" and "no" with their peers and adults. As teens practice these skills, they're also engaging in romantic relationships and curiously questioning their development and sexual health, while navigating gender identity, sexual orientation, and gender expression.

I want to put all of these "normal" developmental experiences into context. If you feel overwhelmed by all of these developmental pieces, I can say with confidence that your teen is overwhelmed, too. I want you to carry this idea with you as you adapt these chapters to real life with your teen. You will undoubtedly have those moments when you feel exhausted by your teen's developmental world, yet I encourage you to take this as an opportunity to discover a curious perspective and ask yourself, "If I'm feeling overwhelmed, how might my teen be feeling?"

So, what are you supposed to do with all of this information? I recommend starting with you. How so? By first answering the stepping-stone questions listed at the beginning of this section. If you actively determine where you stand on these topics, it will be easier to take a concrete approach with supporting your teen daughter. Once you've assessed your baseline position, I would start with those topic areas that either (1) feel like a priority or (2) feel the easiest to address and discuss with your teen.

As you know, each chapter has parenting tools that will help guide you, so once you pick a topic area that makes the most sense for you and your teen, go back and re-read the parenting tips. Next, pick one or two tips to put into practice. Then, you can gradually move toward those sections that feel more difficult to address.

Before you move into practice, please read this next part: *There is no expectation that you master a parenting tip the first time you put it into practice.* In fact, it could take a few times before it feels easy. The more you practice, the more confident you will be, and the more organic these tools will feel. If you get stuck when in practice, no worries—you can always take a step back and resume when you feel ready.

That brings me to another point on these parenting tools. These parenting tips are recommendations, not hard-core templates that need to be followed exactly. Please use your judgment on how to best implement these guidelines for your teen. Don't forget to take a collaborative approach with your teen, as both of you have your own unique perspectives on how to best move forward.

As you move beyond this book, please remember that while the teen years can be challenging, they can also be filled with numerous opportunities for growth. As a therapist, I can empathize with the many layers of adolescence, yet I want loved ones to also embrace these layers as new opportunities to witness your teen changing and finding their own authentic version of who they are in this world. These two things are incredibly important, not only from a developmental perspective, but also from the perspective of your teen.

Unconditionally loving and accepting your teen as they are is what your teen wants most from you, and it's something they will undoubtedly remember and be grateful for long into their adult years. And just like me, your teen doesn't expect you to get it right every single time. Go forth, remain present, and watch as your daughter takes flight on her own unique journey. As it happens, don't forget to celebrate the ways you helped guide, support, and develop that remarkable person within.

RESOURCES

BOOKS

The Awakened Family: How to Raise Empowered, Resilient, and Conscious Children by Shefali Tsabary, PhD

Provides parents with resources on how to raise children to be their authentic selves.

Brainstorm: The Power and Purpose of the Teenage Brain by Daniel J. Siegel, MD

Addresses brain research for individuals between the ages of twelve and twenty-four.

Codependent No More: How to Stop Controlling Others and Start Caring for Yourself by Melody Beattie

A great read for anyone, this book supports parents to create healthy boundaries between their teen and themselves.

Cutting: Understanding and Overcoming Self-Mutilation by Steven Levenkron

Discusses cutting from the perspective of how self-mutilation manifests and explores how individuals can be supported.

The Gifts of Imperfect Parenting: Raising Children with Courage, Compassion, and Connection by Brené Brown

Ties together themes of vulnerability, creativity, and wholeheartedness to support parents and children with 10 guideposts.

Hardwiring Happiness: The New Brain Science of Contentment, Calm, and Confidence by Rick Hanson, PhD

Guided practices to learn simple tools to override the brain's bias for negativity, with sections on children, motivation, and well-being.

Nonviolent Communication: A Language of Life: Life-Changing Tools for Healthy Relationships **by Marshall B. Rosenberg, PhD**

Provides information on conscious communication practices and highlights what "violent" communication is.

Permission to Feel: Unlocking the Power of Emotions to Help Our Kids, Ourselves, and Our Society Thrive **by Marc Brackett, PhD**

Integrates science to help parents and children understand emotions and how to feel them.

Queen Bees and Wannabes: Helping Your Daughter Survive Cliques, Gossip, Boys, and the New Realities of Girl World **by Rosalind Wiseman**

Talks about how females interact socially, navigate friendships, and express their anger.

The Seven Spiritual Laws for Parents: Guiding Your Children to Success and Fulfillment **by Deepak Chopra, MD**

Grounded in love and compassion, this book discusses how these two skills can lead to abundance and success.

The Spiritual Child: The New Science on Parenting for Health and Lifelong Thriving **by Lisa Miller, PhD**

Explores the connection between spirituality and health.

Yoga for Depression: A Compassionate Guide to Relieve Suffering Through Yoga **by Amy Weintraub**

This book presents breathing and meditation practices that help address different moods, not just depression, and provides tools that parents and teens can both use.

WEBSITES

The Australian Parenting Website

RaisingChildren.net.au

Provides articles for parents on different topics including technology, communication, development, and more.

Center for Parent & Teen Communication

ParentandTeen.com

Provides information on multiple topics including growth and development, communication strategies, building character, and health and prevention, and a section for teens.

Futures Without Violence

FuturesWithoutViolence.org

Nonprofit organization with a mission to end domestic and sexual violence. Provides educational resources for teens and caregivers.

The Gottman Institute: A Research-Based Approach to Relationships

Gottman.com

Organization that brings research to relationships and provides resources including information for parents.

The Human Rights Campaign

HRC.org

Globally recognized organization that advocates for LGBTQ+ individuals. Provides resources on many topics, such as parenting, sexual health, and communities of color.

Making Caring Common Project

MCC.GSE.Harvard.edu

Part of the Harvard Graduate School of Education. Provides resources for caregivers, with a mission to create a world with youth who learn to treat others kindly.

National Alliance on Mental Illness (NAMI)

NAMI.org

U.S.-based grassroots organization committed to helping those affected by mental illness. Contains resources for those affected and family members.

National Eating Disorders Association (NEDA)

NationalEatingDisorders.org

Nonprofit dedicated to helping individuals and families impacted by eating disorders.

National Institute on Alcohol Abuse and Alcoholism (NIAAA)

NIAAA.NIH.gov

Provides educational resources driven by research and material on the impact of alcohol on the well-being of individuals.

National Institute on Drug Abuse (NIDA)

DrugAbuse.gov

Provides information regarding drug use prevention and resources for individuals seeking drug treatment.

National Suicide Prevention Lifeline

SuicidePreventionLifeline.org

Toll-free hotline: 1-(800)-273-8255

U.S.-based suicide prevention network for individuals in crisis.

Planned Parenthood Federation of America, Inc.

PlannedParenthood.org

Nonprofit organization that provides reproductive health services in the U.S. and globally.

Stop Bullying

StopBullying.gov

Provides educational and preventative materials and resources for parents on bullying and cyberbullying.

Substance Abuse and Mental Health Services Administration (SAMHSA)

SAMHSA.gov

U.S.-based organization that provides mental health information, resources, and research to the public.

The Trevor Project

TheTrevorProject.org

24/7 toll-free crisis helpline: 1-(866)-488-7386 or text "START" to 678678

Nonprofit organization focused on suicide prevention for lesbian, gay, bisexual, transgender, queer, and questioning youth.

REFERENCES

American Academy of Child & Adolescent Psychiatry. "Teen Brain: Behavior, Problem-Solving, and Decision Making." *American Academy of Child & Adolescent Psychiatry*, September 2016. AACAP.org/AACAP/Families_and_Youth/Facts_for_Families /FFF-Guide/The-Teen-Brain-Behavior-Problem-Solving-and -Decision-Making-095.aspx.

American Psychological Association. "Who Self-Injures?" July/August 2015, vol. 46, no. 7. APA.org/monitor/2015/07-08/who-self-injures.

Arain, Mariam, et al., "Maturation of the Adolescent Brain." *Neuropsychiatric Disease and Treatment*, no. 9, April 2013: 449–461. NCBI.NLM.NIH .gov/pmc/articles/PMC3621648.

Bany-Mohammed, Haneen. "Why Do Girls Mature Faster Than Boys?" *Baron News*. February 28, 2020. BaronNews.com/2020/02/28/why -do-girls-mature-faster-than-boys.

Beauty Schools Directory. "Body Image: List of Facts, Figures, and Statistics." Accessed September 22, 2021. BeautySchoolsDirectory .com/blog/body-image-statistics.

Bergland, Christopher. "Scientists Identify Why Girls Often Mature Faster Than Boys." *Psychology Today*. December 20, 2013. PsychologyToday .com/us/blog/the-athletes-way/201312/scientists-identify-why-girls -often-mature-faster-boys.

Blaha, Michael Joseph, reviewer. "5 Vaping Facts You Need to Know." Johns Hopkins Medicine. Accessed October 15, 2021. HopkinsMedicine.org /health/wellness-and-prevention/5-truths-you-need-to-know-about -vaping.

Bohanon, Mariah. "Activists and Researchers Say School Dress Codes Unfairly Target African American Girls." DiversityIS. March 2, 2020. DiversityIS.com/activists-and-researchers-say-school-dress-codes -unfairly-target-african-american-girls.

Center for Change. "Battling Our Bodies: Understanding and Overcoming Negative Body Images." Accessed September 23, 2021. CenterforChange.com/battling-bodies-understanding-overcoming -negative-body-images.

Center for Discovery. "Eating Disorders in Minorities & Marginalized Groups." Accessed September 22, 2021. CenterforDiscovery .com/blog/causes-for-eating-disorder-minorities.

Chaplin, Tara M., and Amelia Aldao. "Gender Differences in Emotion Expression in Children: A Meta-Analytic Review." *Psychological Bulletin* 139, no. 4, December 2012. NCBI.NLM.NIH.gov/pmc/articles /PMC3597769.

Cherry, Kendra. "What Is Gender Expression?" VerywellMind. October 1, 2021. VerywellMind.com/what-is-gender-expression-5187952.

Cody, Paula. "The Teenage Brain: What Are They Thinking?" UWHealth. June 21, 2018. parenting.UWHealth.org/2018/06/teenage-brain -thinking.

Discovery Mood & Anxiety Program. "Drugs of Abuse: What's the Differ-ence Between Meth, Heroin and Xanax?" Accessed October 14, 2021. DiscoveryMood.com/blog/drugs-abuse-whats-difference-meth -heroin-xanax.

Fleps, Bella. "Social Media Effects on Body Image and Disorders." Illinois State University. April 21, 2021. news.IllinoisState.edu/2021/04 /social-media-effects-on-body-image-and-eating-disorders.

Glick, Anne. "Diverse Friends Are Good for Kids (and Require Confidence!)—Part 2/2." Globe Smart Kids. November 22, 2017. GlobeSmartKids.org/21st-century-skills/diverse-friends-are-good -for-kids-and-require-confidence-part-22.

Gordon, Sherri. "8 Reasons Why Teens Bully Others." VerywellFamily. February 4, 2021. VerywellFamily.com/reasons-why-teens-bully -others-460532.

Healthy Life Recovery. "Vaping Drugs: What Drugs Can Be Vaped?" October 12, 2020. HealthyLifeRecovery.com/vaping-drugs-what -drugs-can-be-vaped.

High Impact. "How Social Media Influences Teens." Accessed September 17, 2021. YouthTrainingSolutions.com/news/how-social-media -influences-teens.

Hudson, Chris. "Mean Girls: Why Teenage Girls Can Be So Cruel." Under-standing Teenagers. September 2012. UnderstandingTeenagers.com .au/mean-girls-why-teenage-girls-can-be-so-cruel.

Jacobson, Rae. "How to Talk to Your Teen About Substance Use." Child Mind Institute. Accessed October 5, 2021. ChildMind.org/article/talk-teenager-substance-use-abuse.

Jenco, Melissa. "Study: 73% of High School Students Not Getting Enough Sleep." *American Academy of Pediatrics*. January 25, 2018. publications.AAP.org/aapnews/news/13792.

Kuchinskas, Susan. "What's Going on Inside Your Teen's Head?" *Grow by WebMD*. March 9, 2011. WebMD.com/parenting/features/inside-look-at-the-teen-brain.

Lisitsa, Ellie. "An Introduction to Emotion Coaching." The Gottman Institute. June 8, 2012. Gottman.com/blog/an-introduction-to-emotion-coaching.

Locker, Melissa. "Boys May Actually Be Meaner Than Girls, Study Says." *TIME*. December 3, 2014. Time.com/3614730/boys-may-actually-be-meaner-than-girls-study-says.

MacDonald, Fiona. "Girls Are Going through Puberty Earlier Than Ever Before, with Long-Term Health Risks." *ScienceAlert*. June 28, 2016. ScienceAlert.com/girls-are-going-through-puberty-earlier-than-ever-before-with-long-term-effects.

Maryville University. "What Is Cyberbullying? Facts, Laws & Resources." Accessed October 1, 2021. online.Maryville.edu/blog/what-is-cyberbullying-an-overview-for-students-parents-and-teachers.

Mayo Clinic Staff. "Teens and Social Media Use: What's the Impact?" Mayo Clinic. December 21, 2019. MayoClinic.org/healthy-lifestyle/tween-and-teen-health/in-depth/teens-and-social-media-use/art-20474437.

Merrill, Stephen. "Decoding the Teenage Brain (in 3 Charts)." Edutopia. January 31, 2019. Edutopia.org/article/decoding-teenage-brain-3-charts.

Miller, Caroline. "Why You Should Be Talking to Teens About Sex." Child Mind Institute. Accessed September 24, 2021. ChildMind.org/article/why-you-should-have-frank-sex-talks-with-teens.

Moritz, Troy. "Vaping: It's All Smoke and Mirrors." American Lung Association. March 18, 2019. Lung.org/blog/vaping-smoke-and-mirrors.

National Center for Drug Abuse Statistics. "Drug Use among Youth: Facts & Statistics." Accessed October 5, 2021. DrugAbuseStatistics.org /teen-drug-use.

National Eating Disorders Association. "People of Color and Eating Disorders." Accessed September 22, 2021. NationalEatingDisorders .org/people-color-and-eating-disorders.

National Institute of Mental Health. "Eating Disorders." Accessed September 21, 2021. NIMH.NIH.gov/health/statistics/eating-disorders.

National Institute on Drug Abuse. "Vaping Devices (Electronic Cigarettes) DrugFacts." January 2020. DrugAbuse.gov/publications /drugfacts/vaping-devices-electronic-cigarettes.

Newport Academy. "The Importance of Teen Friendships." July 2, 2018. NewportAcademy.com/resources/empowering-teens/teen -friendships.

Norton, Amy. "Why Today's Teens Are Growing Up More Slowly Than They Used To." *CBS News*. September 19, 2017. CBSNews.com/news /why-todays-teens-are-growing-up-more-slowly-than-they-used-to.

Planned Parenthood. "Abstinence-Only-Until-Marriage Programs." Accessed September 24, 2021. PlannedParenthoodAction.org/issues/sex -education/abstinence-only-programs.

Planned Parenthood. "Sex Education Laws and State Attacks." Accessed September 24, 2021. PlannedParenthoodAction.org/issues /sex-education/sex-education-laws-and-state-attacks.

RaisingChildren.net.au. "Brain Development in Pre-Teens and Teenagers." Accessed September 3, 2021. RaisingChildren.net.au/pre-teens /development/understanding-your-pre-teen/brain-development -teens.

Revenga, Ana, and Sudhir Shetty. "Empowering Women Is Smart Economics." *Finance & Development*. 49, no. 1, March 2012. IMF.org/external/pubs/ft/fandd/2012/03/revenga.htm.

Richards, Patti. "How Does Media Impact Body Image and Eating Disorder Rates?" Center for Change. Accessed September 25, 2021. CenterforChange.com/how-does-media-impact-body-image-and -eating-disorder-rates.

Safe at Last. "28 Captivating Teen Driving Statistics [2021]—Safe at Last."
    June 25, 2021. SafeatLast.co/blog/teen-driving-statistics/#gref.

Sandoiu, Ana. "Strong Friendships in Adolescence May Benefit Mental
    Health in the Long Run." *Medical News Today*. August 26, 2017.
    MedicalNewsToday.com/articles/319119.

Sifferlin, Alexandra. "Why Teenage Brains Are So Hard to Understand."
    TIME. September 8, 2017. Time.com/4929170/inside-teen
    -teenage-brain.

Stanford Children's Health. "Cognitive Development in the Teen Years."
    Accessed September 2, 2021. StanfordChildrens.org/en/topic
    /default?id=cognitive-development-90-P01594.

Stetka, Bret. "Extended Adolescence: When 25 Is the New 18." *Scientific
    American*. September 19, 2017. ScientificAmerican.com/article
    /extended-adolescence-when-25-is-the-new-181.

Stop Bullying. "What Is Cyberbullying." Accessed October 2, 2021.
    StopBullying.gov/cyberbullying/what-is-it.

Talk It Out. "Get the Facts about Alcohol & the Teenage Brain." Accessed
    October 15, 2021. TalkItOutNC.org/alcohol-developing-brain.

University of New England. "How to Ask for Enthusiastic Consent."
    December 27, 2019. UNELife.com.au/blog/2019/12/27/how-to
    -ask-for-enthusiastic-consent.

University of Rochester Medical Center. "Understanding the Teen Brain."
    Accessed August 31, 2021. URMC.rochester.edu/encyclopedia
    /content.aspx?ContentTypeID=1&ContentID=3051.

World Health Organization. "Adolescent Mental Health." November 17,
    2021. WHO.int/news-room/fact-sheets/detail/adolescent
    -mental-health.

INDEX

Fight or flight response,
23, 114–115
Friendships
"bad influences," 51–52
diversity in, 49–51
engaging with, 57
importance of strong,
48–49, 59
Frontal cortex, 23, 24

G

Gender expression, 97–100,
105–106, 107
Gender-fluid, 98
Gender inequality, 8, 13, 14
Gender norms, 99–100
Gender roles, 98
Gender stereotypes, 99–100
GIFs, 38
Gottman, John, xi
Group chats, 38

H

Hippocampus, 114
Hormones, 18
Hypothalamus, 114–115

I

Identity exploration, 12, 96–97,
105–108. *See also* Gender
expression; Self-expression
Inclusivity, in school dress
codes, 11
Indirect aggression, 35–36, 42
Individuality, 4–5
Influences on teens, 2–3, 13–14
Interests, 97

L

LGBTQ+ sex education,
86–87, 88, 90
Life skills, learning, 6, 12
Limbic system, 23, 24

M

Marijuana, 117, 120, 124
Maturation, girls vs. boys,
19–20, 29
Meanness, 35–36.
See also Bullying
Memes, 37–38
Menstruation, 18, 21–22
Mental health concerns,
25–26, 100–101, 107
Milestones, 5–6

N

"No," saying, 122

O

Online validation, 38–39
Opioids, 117

P

Parent, use of term, x
Parenting myths and misnomers,
6–8, 12–13, 14
Parties, 115–116
Peer pressure, 96, 107,
122, 124, 127
Photo sharing sites, 37
Physical changes,
18, 21–22, 26–27
Positive parenting,
ix, x–xi, 127–129
Prefrontal cortex, 23, 24, 112, 114
Problem-solving skills, 28, 49
Pronouns, 98
Pruning, 22–24, 29
Puberty, 18, 20, 21–22, 26–27, 29

R

Rejection, 53
Relationships
abusive, 55
dating, 52–56, 57–58, 59–60
friendships, 48–52, 57, 59

Relationships (*continued*)
  healthy, 54–55
  templates for, 58
Risk-taking behaviors,
    23–24, 27, 29, 114–115

S

Self-expression, 102–105.
    See also Identity exploration
Self-harming behaviors, 67–69
Sex
  abstinence-only
    programs, 87–88
  and consent, 54, 81–82
  conversations about,
    54, 58–59, 83–84, 89–90
  education, 84–85,
    87–88, 90–92
  importance of talking
    about, 80–81
  non-heterosexual, 86–87
Sexting, 40
Sexual orientation, 99
Social changes, 19
Social media
  and body image, 72–73, 77
  cyberbullying,
    66–67, 68–69, 75, 77

establishing expectations
    for use of, 43
  forms of, 36–38, 45
  and pressure to perform,
    38–39, 43, 44
  risks of, 40–41, 45
  and teen culture, 2
Social networking, 37
Stimulants, 117
Substance use
  abuse and addiction, 123
  alcohol, 112–116, 124
  drugs, 116–119, 124
  vaping, 119–120, 125

T

Teen culture, 2–6, 13–14
Texting, 32

U

Uniqueness, 4–5

V

Vaping, 119–120, 125
Video sharing sites, 37
Vlogging, 38
Vulnerability, 33, 54

ACKNOWLEDGMENTS

Thank you to my parents, Joe and Sylvia Trujillo, for unconditionally supporting me and for always believing in, and pushing me in the direction of, my dreams. Laura Long, my business coach, thank you for sharing my name. Without you, this book wouldn't be a reality. Juliet Oliver, thank you for being my cheerleader throughout this process. Our morning conversations were a saving grace when I doubted myself. To Missy Fowler, my voice was lost for some time; thank you for reminding me to speak my authentic truth. Megan Zuzevich, thank you for holding space for me to process, literally, everything. Your insights guided me to step into my strength; no more playing small. Erin Ferrell, thank you for always having my back, the many moments of laughter, and talking big picture with me. To my brother, Joey Trujillo, thank you for being you. I've learned so much from you.

ABOUT THE AUTHOR

 **CHRISTINA TRUJILLO SIEREN**, LCSW, was born and raised near Los Angeles, California. Growing up, she was fascinated by human behavior and how the mind worked. Turning her passion into a career, Christina now owns a private practice as a licensed psychotherapist, working with high-risk adolescents and families. In 2021, she opened Unapparent Parenting, Inc., where she provides coaching for parents of teens, supporting caregivers to explore and connect with their most authentic selves. Christina believes that parenting is a journey that is uniquely challenging and filled with endless experiences to witness our children as they are. Christina has a burning curiosity and loves learning. You can easily find her reading or taking up a new hobby.